of OLLI

Thank you!

2MV

as Minh Fullerton

14 March 2015

Thank You,

America!

Minh Fullerton

ISBN: 978-1-941125-31-1

Library 0f Congress Control Number: 2015934338

Acknowledgement

I wish to express my special thanks to Marcella Lorfing, my Memoir Teacher at OLLI (Osher Life Long Institute, UC Davis Extension) and the class for making this book possible. All of the seventeen stories in Part One were critiqued and corrected by them. Story number one through seven should be read in order. Other stories can be read individually.

Forty years ago, I lost everything on the last day of April 1975 when the Vietnam War ended. I became a war criminal with all the consequences followed. Now I am a free man.

As the title says it, this little book is my deep gratitude to the American people who rescued me from Communism in 1993. Without the American spirit of Freedom and Humanitarianism, I would not have a second chance with my life. I am so proud to be an American citizen.

Minh Fullerton

March 2015

i

CONTENTS

---***---

Part One   *Stories of My Prime Years in Darkness,*
1975-1985

1.	The Sleepless Tuesday of 1975	*1*
2.	The Big Catch	*8*
3.	The Flight into Darkness	*16*
4.	The Dungeon Game, Part 1	*23*
5.	The Dungeon Game, Part 2	*29*
6.	Down to The Bottom, Part 1	*37*
7.	Down to The Bottom, Part 2	*42*
8.	Message Understood	*47*
9.	Breaking Up an Antenna	*54*
10.	Family Visits	*60*
11.	Was It Love?	*68*
12.	The Small Catch	*76*
13.	Choosing The Wrong Door	*83*
14.	The Grave Digger	*88*
15.	The Wild Plum	*94*
16.	The Beginning of True Love	*101*

Misc: The Double Ugly Ducklings   *108*

Poem: Black April   *115*

Part Two   *My Journey to Freedom*   *117-164*

:

Part One:

Stories of My Prime Years in Darkness,

1975-1985

1- The Sleepless Tuesday of 1975

Early on Tuesday, 29th of April 1975, I heard the announcement loudly and repeatedly on Saigon radio, requesting all Americans to leave Saigon within 24 hours. For me and others working at the South Vietnam Central Intelligence Organization (SVN/CIO), the secret code was the song "White Christmas" by Bing Crosby on the American radio channel for the final evacuation. I soon heard the song while I was on duty. I was given two hours to go home and pack up for the rendezvous at 5:00 PM. In my naïve and idealistic mind, I thought things were still in order as planned. I was so wrong…

Along with Dieu, my girlfriend, I bowed twice and begged for forgiveness from her parents. I then shook hands to say goodbye to Kham, her brother, who was my close friend in college, before I hurriedly took Dieu on my mini scooter to the rendezvous point. I took her to a safe house of the SVN/CIO. This one was on Nguyen Hau Street, the street behind the Central Post Office, a few blocks from the US Embassy. Saigon was in total chaos as the helicopters, big and small, from the US Seven Fleet were crowding the sky noisily to begin the final withdrawal. The government PA system announced incessantly the 24/7 curfew on the entire city, but the chaotic commotion and the exploding panic of the people were noisier and louder. The End was coming in a big way.

"We have the plan to evacuate the CIO and family members," the CIA liaison official assured that in the last meeting more than a week earlier. I submitted my girlfriend's name after discussing the probable outcome with her family once the Communists took over: I would be executed and she would be forced to marry a disabled Viet Cong. With her parents' reluctant approval, she and I went to a jewelry store to buy a set of engagement rings. Once I heard the coded song on that Tuesday, I rushed to her brother's home and signaled her to leave. She was like a frightened little bird leaving her warm nest going out to the stormy unknown sky. She was only nineteen, eight years younger than I was.

Dieu had been my girlfriend since I frequented her brother's home in 1973. She was seventeen then. She was sent from her parents' home in the fishing village of Phuoc Hai to Saigon to go to high school. I loved her slender youthfulness and the long, black silky hair touching playfully on her shoulders. I loved her distinct seaside voice, especially when she giggled. I loved her cooking, too. I was taking time to show my love and she made the first move. One night, as I was alone upstairs reading, Dieu came up with some cookies. She took one into her mouth, came and turned me around then shared the cookie with me. It became a frantic kiss as I stood up and hugged her tight. As I held her face in my hands, I looked into her jet black eyes and said: "I love you," she broke loose timidly and hurriedly ran away. She turned back quickly to give me the most beautiful smile before

2

she disappeared downstairs. I was in high clouds and my heart was beating fast for a long while. Wow!

Dieu and I started having secret dates after that first kiss. I usually took one afternoon off work during the week to go to the movies with her; of course she had to play hooky for that. Our love grew stronger and deeper with time, but we had a mutual agreement that we saved the best of our love for the wedding night. I was taught by my mother that sex was not for fun, that virginity was the girl's sacred thing. Besides, I could not betray the trust that Kham and Dieu's parents had on me. I wanted to step into her family the righteous way as my mother kept reminding me and expected me to do.

The rendezvous point was already crowded when I led Dieu in after we passed the security check point. Once inside, I left Dieu in a room. I had to report to my supervisor first. It took me a couple of minutes to find my supervisor and others in my unit in a big conference room.

"We go as a unit," said he. "We are expected to resume working as soon as we are safely in America."

I could feel the tension of Dieu's grip on my left arm when I rejoined her. It was surely not a good way to introduce my girlfriend to my work place. Adults were mixing with children. People were all over the desks and chairs. Suitcases, backpacks, and handbags were everywhere. Dieu and I settled down next to our handbags in a corner as the room was getting more crowded. Everyone exchanged greetings, mixing words of hope and anxiety.

I noticed that some people didn't show up. Some, I was told, left earlier for the US Embassy on their own because they had connections. Some stayed put hoping they could get promoted in the new government which could be accepted by the Communists. Rumors spread that a new government was in the making. It would consist of three elements: the Communist, the neutral, and the pro-Western one. For me, I made up my mind to be loyal to my unit and I would accept the fate of "going down with the ship" although I pretty much hoped that it wouldn't be that way.

After wearing the engagement rings, I held Dieu's hands firmly and assured her. I tried to convince her as well as myself:

"Darling, don't worry. We'll be leaving soon."

"How?" asked Dieu, with a trembling voice.

"Perhaps we'll be escorted to the embassy. I don't see anywhere a helicopter could land here."

My guess was as good as anybody's guess. The safe house was a big old building with tiled roof. There was no big yard inside its iron fence. The streets around it were full of people on cars and motorcycles going in all directions. I could hear helicopters hovering and passing by above the building on their way to the embassy. The whole scene was surreal as in a war movie.

Everyone was waiting for the signal from Mr. NPL, the Chief of the CIO to leave the building. He was in a front room with his immediate staff, trying frantically to contact the US Embassy. From the position of the Deputy Chief of Planning, Mr. NPL became the Chief of the CIO just over a week earlier. The former chief, a two-star general, fled when Mr. Thieu, the former President of South Vietnam fled on April 21. That general was Mr. Thieu's trusted relative. Being the Chief of both the CIO and the National Police Forces, that general had secured the power grip for Mr. Thieu. He had to go when Mr. Thieu deserted his people.

Midnight passed. Everybody was sleepless. Everybody was very much holding their breath in the building. Tension mounted. Anxiety heightened. The city outside was sleepless with all the panicky noise and chaos, too.

As we still had no contact with the US embassy, Mr. NPL decided to make a move. He sent his Deputy Chief of Operations, a colonel, to the embassy. Everybody waited, and hoped, and prayed. I told Dieu to scoot down onto the floor so she could rest her head on the handbag and close her eyes a bit while I was watching. A sense of uncertainty was growing in my mind and I silently prayed for the worst not to come. I sensed my heavy responsibility for Dieu's well-being. Gosh, this is a brave girl who left her family for love, how could I fail her…

The early light of dawn was seeping into every room in the building and still no word came from the colonel. The frequency of the helicopters became less and less. We all became restless and were losing hope fast. All sleepless eyes became weary, tired and staring blank into the grey sky. Everybody was afraid to say the bad, bad word: No evacuation.

Around 6:00 AM of Wednesday, April 30, Mr. NPL hung up the phone after his last attempt to contact the embassy. He then called an impromptu meeting of his staff. He spoke with a controlled calmness:

"I lose all hope of evacuation. The Americans have abandoned us. You now can leave on your own. I am sorry for failing you. I am staying with the ship as we still have the government. Go as you wish. Good luck. Goodbye!"

I returned to where Dieu was waiting for me. She saw my teary eyes and she broke into tears herself. I was helpless in consoling her. I was speechless at the moment. We picked up our handbags and left the building on foot as I could not find my scooter anywhere. The walk home was about two hours, through chaotic streets. I was so absorbed in my bleak future that all I could remember was the empty grey sky without any sunshine. I was numb and dragging my feet like a walking corpse. I couldn't remember if I was holding Dieu's hand or not.

I tried to gather myself at her brother's home. I reasoned to her that we still had a government, as my superior said. Maybe the Communists would accept a three-element government as a peaceful solution then I still would have the job. I spoke and tried to look into her eyes but Dieu avoided looking at me. She was facing a big problem of her own: Leaving her parents without a proper marriage.

At about 10:30 AM on that Wednesday of the Black April 1975, General Big Minh, the three-day President of South Vietnam announced his total surrender to the Communists on the radio. South Vietnam ceased to exist. The announcement came as I was having a bowl of noodle soup. The noodles suddenly became bitter and so coarse in my throat that I had to give up eating. I stared blankly into the wall. I stopped hearing sounds around me. I was sinking down fast to an unknown bottom…

Sinking with the ship was the Chief of the SVN/CIO and my immediate superior, the director of Intelligence Research. Both of them died in concentration camps in North Vietnam. I was in the same camps with them from the south to the north.

<1>

2- The Big Catch

"Goodbye, darling. I'll see you in a month. Be strong."

Those were my last words to Dieu, my fiancée. We were holding hands and looking at each other. I could feel my voice was not convincing as tears were in my fiancée's eyes and she was biting her lips. I let go of her hands and turned to leave her. After a few steps, I looked back to see Dieu riding the mini-bicycle away. The streets were still quiet and empty at noon time. Uncertainty seemed to hang in the air. Saigon, which now had a new name as Ho Chi Minh City, just had the new government over a month. I wanted to grasp the last image of the surroundings before I walked through the big metal gate of CHU VAN AN High School, where I was ordered to report for re-education.

The day was June 15, 1975, forty six days after the collapse of South Vietnam, formally known as the Republic of Vietnam (RVN). The notice to report for re-education was from the Military Management Committee of Ho Chi Minh City. It gave former high-ranking government officials, like me and former middle to high ranking military officers three days, June 13 to June 15, to report at designated locations throughout the city. I chose to report on the last day because I was lingering with my fiancée. I just got engaged two weeks earlier.

I was a high ranking intelligence official in the South Vietnam government. My organization was left behind. The planned evacuation was aborted due to extreme chaos in the last hours at the US Embassy. My colleagues and I had no choice but to accept what was coming to us from the victors. The first Communist words about people who worked in the old regime were "National reconciliation" and "Revolutionary leniency." So far, there was no blood bath as I anticipated. I started believing the words from the Communists when I heard them with my own ears from the mouth of my long-lost cousin. He came back from the North as a colonel in the Liberation Army of the Provisional Revolutionary Government of Republic of South Vietnam.

I remembered two weeks ago that I was happy to receive the news for re-education. I saw it as the first step to rebuild my new life. My old life as an intelligence agent was gone. I had lost my job, my income and my future. All I had left was my fiancée and my family. They were relieved that I was not executed. They were happy to see me go for re-education. The notice instructed me to bring belongings and money for one month. Yes, only one month then I would be back with my loved ones. I was eager to go for re-education to get it over with. I brought with me a big handbag of clothes, a piece of tarp as a mat, a light blanket, a raincoat and a mosquito net. My second bag was a small, square one with toiletries, some medicine and a towel. The small bag would be used as my pillow. My parents gave me money more than enough for a month payment but I only took some extra money, "just in case I need to call a Pedi cab to go home." In my small bag, my fiancée gave me 30 pieces of candy for 30 days I was away from her.

"The month of June has 30 days", she said, "I don't give you any extra because I am your candy when you're back." She cheered me up with her seductive voice.

And I promised her that I would come right back to taste her again...

Everything seemed surreal behind the gate of CHU VAN AN High School. I was in line to register for re-education. On the other side of the table was a young militia with a red band on his right arm. He read what I filled out in the questionnaire to the army officer standing by him. The young militia seemed puzzled while reading my personal history. He was too young to know about my title: Bureau Chief of Intelligence Research on North Vietnam Politics. On the contrary, I could detect a scolding from the Communist army officer.

Once the registration was done, I was told to pay money for a month of meals then wait until a group of ten was formed. My group of ten was sent to a classroom on the second floor of the third and last building. I settled my belongings down on a vacant space on the floor, next to one of my former employees. The classroom was full in an hour with about forty people. More than half chose the floor; the rest had to sleep on the long tables. The atmosphere in the classroom was very weird because everyone was present but not in working attire and not working. Everyone was present but no one was superior or subordinate. Everyone was equally stripped to nothing. I heard someone's remark:

"We start our new life again as a student, how appropriate to be in this high school!"

I found the striking fact was very hard to swallow.

For the evening of June 15 and the following two days, I was impressed with the Communist treatment. I was free to roam inside the high school; no class was given. For meals, my colleagues and I were given the food from a well-known restaurant in Saigon. Wow! That special feeling was multiplied when I saw the way the Communist soldiers ate. They did not eat the food from the restaurant. They cooked their own meals instead. They did the cooking in front of us. I saw them eat only rice with vegetables. I heard someone, on behalf of the re-educationees, offered them a portion of the restaurant food.

"No, thank you." The officer answered with a smile, "You paid money for your food, so you enjoy it. Revolutionary Ethics do not allow us to eat your food."

I liked that Revolutionary ethics! "That's why they won the war." I thought.

At 2:00 AM on June 18, 1975, I experienced for the first time the Communist tactic of moving at night. Everyone in the high school was ordered to get up and pack up. Nobody dared to ask about destination because the Communist troupe ordered everyone to be quiet and they had their weapons ready to shoot. They swiftly went back and forth and around the herd of people who were told to sit still in the middle of the school yard. I was in that herd. I felt like I was cattle that were being rounded up for sale or for meat. Light was at minimum. The soldiers were going around with flashlights. Early morning chill added suspense to the tense atmosphere. I was about to go on an unknown path.

Around 4:00 AM, I heard the rumbling sound of commercial buses coming into the school yard. The buses were loaded quickly with one soldier by the driver and one in the back of each bus. Once inside the bus, I was told to look straight, be still and quiet during the trip. The soldiers did not say anything else. All the window blinds on the bus were shut down. Darkness came at dawn. Like others, I was trying to figure out where the buses were going in the darkness. Definitely we were taken out of Saigon, my beloved city, but where? I wished I had been sitting behind the driver. Nobody was sure of anything anymore.

After about two hours, the buses finally slowed down and made a sharp turn uphill. I heard surprised words from the front row, "Long Thanh Orphanage Village!" The soldiers didn't seem to mind the noise anymore, and they didn't care when the person next to me lifted the blind on the window. The buses rolled slowly between rows of brick buildings and stopped. What used to be

"Long Thanh Orphanage Village" was now "Long Thanh Re-education camp." "How ironic!" I thought. I had become an orphan after I lost my fatherland.

Long Thanh camp was on a hill, about 50 miles east of Saigon. I was among 2,000 persons who were transported there for re-education. I learned later that there were four blocks in the camp: The Intelligence block (which I was in), the Central government block (included an ex-Prime Minister), the Police Force block, and the Parties block (consisted of central committee members of all former political parties). The core of the South Vietnam government was rounded up.

The rest of the first 30 days went by rather fast. Every day I had meetings in groups to read state-run newspapers. Every night I had self-criticism and self-evaluation sessions in teams (a group consisted of five teams; a team consisted of 10 persons). I was specifically eager to learn about Revolutionary Ethics. I wanted to become a new person in the new socialist society.

On the night of July 14, 1975 everyone packed up, ready to go home the next morning although the camp management officers didn't mention anything. I was somewhat sleepless. Morning came. Nothing happened, just another day as usual; then came another day as usual. I felt like a deflated balloon. Somebody was daring enough to ask a camp officer and he was silent; he just gave us a half smile. "What is going on? My payment for meals is up; I don't have money to pay for another month," I wondered, and I was not alone in those thoughts.

The next morning, everyone was gathered to the big meeting hall. Excitement came alive. Anticipation of good news was spread fast while waiting for the chief of the camp. Everyone was waiting for him to say the magic word and I heard:

> "You should not be worried about paying for your meals. Your payment was used up. From now on, the People's government is taking care of you."

Then he raised his voice:

> "You committed bloody crimes to the people but the Revolutionary government is treating you with leniency. Settle down. You will go home when you are deemed having satisfactory progress in re-education."

I didn't really hear the rest of his speech. I only heard voices around me: "We are fish in their big catch! We are a bunch of fools to believe in what the Communists say!"

On the way back to my sleeping space, I saw the presence of more soldiers. They were less friendly and more watchful. I sat down on my tarp and unpacked my belongings. Suddenly I realized that the chief didn't mention anything about writing to my family.

The next day, I learned the new rules of the camp:

1/ I have to call all of the Communist officers and soldiers as "cadre"

2/ I have to be in standing straight position, three meters (about 3 yards) away from the cadre when speaking to them. My arms must be rigid along my body, no arm movement allowed

3/ I will have to do manual work to produce food for myself. It is called "Re-education through labor" because I had been a "parasite of the society"

4/ I am not allowed to have any contacts with the outside world until further notice

5/ I will have to write and confess all of my crimes against the people

6/ I will report anyone who has anti-Revolutionary activities

7/ Any violations to the rules will be considered as "Anti-Revolutionary" and will be prosecuted.

The Communist concentration game began. It lasted ten years for me; seventeen years for the last one out of prison.

I lost track of how many times I whispered this verse and sent it in the wind to my fiancée:

"Fare thee well! And if forever,
    Still forever, fare thee well:"

(By Lord Byron, 1816)

<2>

3- The Flight into Darkness

Light and noise suddenly woke me up in the middle of a quiet night in October 1976. The commotion was everywhere in the entire Long Thanh camp of about 2,000 political prisoners. Cadres and guards were standing in the yard outside every hall. I followed the order to come out in teams and groups. My name was called to step aside. A few more were also called. The cadre beamed his flashlight on my face with a harsh order:

> "You go back in to collect all you belongings and report to me in ten minutes. You are moving."

I felt a chill in my spine. Moving in the middle of the night was certainly not a good sign. People gave me pitiful glances as I came back out with my handbags.

The selected few, including me, were escorted to the big meeting hall of the camp. Along the way, I noticed the light in each hall was turned off again as a few were escorted out. I realized secrecy was the name of the game. Inside the meeting hall, I heard a voice ending the count at 40. The command post had chosen 40 persons for this moving. I was among the few from the central intelligence block. Others came from the central government block, the police force block, and the party block. Those were the four blocks that made up the core of the South Vietnam government that had been rounded up into Long Thanh camp for "re-education" since June 1975.

What came next seemed so illogical and unreal. I heard the cadre's voice but I could hardly see him in the dark:

> "Before you get on the bus, you will be handcuffed. This is for your safety because people hate you. They will attack the bus if they see you; therefore, we need to protect you. Do not resist. Any resistance will make things worse for you. Do not worry about your luggage. We will load it on the bus for you."

I got on the Communist army bus with a troubled heart. Never before was I in handcuffs, so were the other 39 persons. I could hear heavy sighs here and there. Some were in tears...

The bus left Long Thanh camp in the direction to Saigon. Along the way, I noticed soldiers standing guard every few hundred meters [1 meter= 1.09 yard]. They exchanged flashlight signals with the guards on the bus. The loud engine noise, the rattling sound due to rough road, the trees and plants flashing by the bus windows in the dark, and the bumpy motion made the trip look like in a war movie I had seen before. No, I was not in a movie. I was a prisoner of war for real. I had no idea where I was heading in darkness...

The bus unloaded me and others at Thu Duc Correctional Center in the suburb of Saigon. I now came into a real prison with thick walls and iron bars. After I identified my belongings, I was led into a cell of ten inmates before my handcuffs were unlocked and my luggage was given back to me. My first impression of the cell was the stench. It was a mixture of smells of concrete, sweat, urine and human waste. As dawn was creeping through the iron bars, I could see more clearly that I was in confinement. Food was shoved in twice a day through a little window like a bird cage. The door was locked all day. I was told no bathing as it was a weekday. My cellmates were former police officers and army officers of high ranks, lieutenant colonel and colonel. Some came to Thu Duc prison just a day earlier. I realized this was a selected round-up for something not good. The worst thing could happen was execution. "Que sera sera," I was thinking, I had already lost control of my life after I reported for "re-education" the year before. I was a kite that was cut loose and blowing in the wind.

I didn't have to wait long. In my second night at Thu Duc prison, I was ordered to get up in the middle of the night again. The whole cell was ordered out to the big yard in the center of buildings. The yard was quickly filled up with more than a hundred prisoners, in darkness. I was told to display everything I had on the ground. A cadre came to me with a flashlight and took away what he deemed unnecessary, such as bottles, cans, all kinds of containers and beddings. He took things away until I could fit the rest of my belongings into one handbag. The other cadres did the same to other prisoners. The noise was loud and rather funny. It was a mixture of yelling, whining and sound of metal things and plastic things being thrown away. Klang, kling, klong, kling, klang, klong. What a loss for those people who liked to collect things…

The army buses, which were heavily guarded, took me and others around and around the skirt of Saigon in darkness before it entered the military airfield of Tan Son Nhat Airport. They finally stopped at the end of a landing strip. I barely made out the silhouettes of the Communist soldiers standing on top of the surrounding hangars. The hangars were covered with layers of sandbags and the soldiers were standing guard in pairs, back to back, facing opposite directions.   One soldier had his rifle pointing at the buses. The other one had his rifle pointing out to the airport perimeter. The atmosphere was deadly tense. I was ordered to stand on the landing strip and form a double line with my handbag on one side. The cadres came between the lines and handcuffed my right hand to the left hand of the other prisoner. I had one hand free to carry my handbag. So did others. It was still dark when I was told I could sit down and relax, but no talking. Of course my partner in handcuff had to do the same thing in unison. We quickly became friends. After a while, the cold air of the morning seeped in everyone's clothes. When a partner needed to go pee, the other had to go with him. The needy act was done standing in the open air a few yards away from the crowd so the guards could keep an eye on things. Who cared about a person's decency when he was considered a war criminal?

In the very early morning light, I heard the sound then I saw two airplanes coming slowly on a taxi way. I could make out only the shape of the C-130 Hercules and its dark green color. I'll never forget the feeling of getting on the C-130. I used to fly in the same kind of plane as a special agent, with soldiers around as my bodyguards. Now I came on board as a prisoner. How bitter and ironic! I took a quick look around and saw tears in many eyes. I was not alone in bitterness. The bitterness was even more as I saw the Communist officers and soldiers came on board with Honda motorcycles, television sets, electric fans, and more. Things they could never have had they not won the war. They were chatting happily in their Northerner's accent. Their voices cut through me like a sharp knife. To see a defeat in a war movie was so different from witnessing my own defeat in front of my own eyes. I had raw, just raw feelings for years.

As the plane flew, I tried to guess where I was heading. The sunlight casting through the windows indicated that I was heading north. The longer the flight, the less familiar became the landscape below. Mixing in the noise of the airplane, I heard a whisper nearby me: "We are definitely leaving the south. The landscape turned grayish and I don't see buildings anymore." That guess came true when the plane landed. I saw a few MIG fighters out of a window, then a Communist officer who hitch-hiked along gave us a victorious smile: "Welcome to our Socialist land of the North! This is Gia Lam Airport in the outskirt of Hanoi."

From the airport, I was herded onto one of the ancient buses made in Soviet Union. All the window blinds were tight-shut. The handcuffs were still on, for my safety of course. The security seemed relaxed with only a police officer on the bus. The Communists seemed confident that people like me could do no harm in their territory. I was sitting behind the driver this time. Everything looked different, and strange. The bus passed Long Bien Bridge over the Red River. An overwhelmingly sad sensation came over me as the bus was rolling on the span that was rebuilt after the American bombers destroyed it. All the war effort was just meaningless. Here and there I saw people pointing fingers at me. I could hear their cursing. Some even threw rocks. I swallowed hard the bitter taste of defeat.

The buses came to the destination at Ha Tay camp, 30 miles southwest of Hanoi. The key to my handcuffs was misplaced. My partner and I were the last ones going through the side gate after the handcuffs were unlocked. Darkness came at noon. I was put in a ward of 60 persons. I began my prison life wearing blue prison clothes for the first time. My number was CT 853[1] on the back of my prison shirt. How wrong I was when I

---

[1] *CT was the abbreviations for either Cai Tao (Re-education) or Chinh Tri (Political). The criminal prisoners did not have CT before their numbers.*

thought that was the worst moment. My darkest months in confinement were waiting for me…

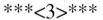

4- The Dungeon Game, Part One: The Setting

As Fate unfolded, I was flown to Ha Tay camp, North Vietnam in October 1976. I was put in Ward number 1, Section A. Roughly a month later, Fate selected me again for something even more special. I was about to be in confinement where the American POWs once were kept. Let the dungeon game begin...

At the time to lock the prisoners up one day, I was singled out by the guard:

> "You take your belongings, including the straw mat to report to Comrade T. here."

Seeing a security police captain with the closing guard was unusual, but now I knew why. He had come for me. Sunlight was fading as I stood with him watching the roll call then people started walking past me to enter the ward. Some people quickly waved their hands in silence. Most of them just gave me a goodbye glance.

I was stunned. Why was I singled out? The highest ranking person in the ward was the Minister sans portfolio, who used to be the head of the South Vietnam team in the Paris Peace Talk. Why me instead of him? Well, I earned the ironic title "Highly-talented young man" since that day. I was only 28 years old, one of the two youngest men in the ward.

The captain led me on foot in the dark with his flashlight. I didn't know where I was going because I turned left and right so many times. I just knew for sure that I didn't leave the camp. I felt I was going deeper inside the camp because I was going between the rough brick walls here and there and the path was muddy. Once in a while the captain had to pause and take my hand to help me jump over a puddle of murky water. The walk was well over 15 minutes to confuse me. It was just five minutes when I was returned to the ward 14 months later.

Finally, Captain T. stopped and unlocked a heavy, big gate with the metal bar crossing it diagonally. I stepped on some dirt before I stood on the concrete foot step in front of a door. Again he had to unlock the door and lifted another metal bar crossing it horizontally. He opened the door wide and signaled with his eyes to order me in. I thought I saw a faint smile on his bony face under the dim light in the cell. Somehow, I didn't feel it was a mean smile. I felt he was just doing his routine job and he welcomed me into his section. He was the warden of Section F, Ha Tay camp.

The door shut loudly behind me with the sound of padlocks echoed twice and the sound of metal bars sliding twice. I walked sideway slowly against the wall to the empty space at the end of the cell. Obviously the five persons who came before me were notified of my coming and they saved me a space next to the toilet. The space was about 1m x 2ms on the concrete platform of 0.5 m high [1 meter= 39.3 inches]. I awkwardly spread out my straw mat, placed my belongings on the mat, and looked around. I nodded in silence as my eyes met the eyes of each person in the cell. All five of them were at least ten years older than I was. Nobody smiled. Dead silence filled the stagnant air. I noticed the smell of newly whitewashed walls. The cell was certainly prepared quite recently for us newcomers. I wanted to be friendly so I started to say Hi to my neighbor. His reaction surprised me:

"SSHHH…" He made the sound with a finger on his mouth, then he pointed to the wall and whispered:

"Don't talk loud. Microphone is in the wall."

My neighbor had come a few days earlier with others from another camp. On the second day, they were secretly warned by the kitchen people who brought them food about the thick yet hollow wall. That explained the dead silence. Soon I heard the faint night bell from the command post. I set up my mosquito net with the help of my neighbor. I lay down on the mat and felt the coldness of concrete creeping into my body. My mind was as numb as my body. The light went off. Welcome to the dungeon.

In the dungeon with me was Brigadier General Nhu, the last police chief of South Vietnam, two police colonels and two special police lieutenant colonels. I was at the lowest rank. My position as a bureau chief was equivalent to a major. I felt a weird, unexpected honor to be in the same cell with a general. Being his partner sometimes in daily and weekly chores to keep the cell clean was even weirder. Captain T. kept track of the rotation. He was present and watchful at every chore to make sure everyone shared the duties equally. No more superiors or subordinates. I came to have great respect for General Nhu as he swallowed the humiliation with dignity. Not all fallen South Vietnamese dignitaries had good manner like he did. Some were whiners and some were just miserable to be around 24 hours a day. Luckily I was moved to different cells every few months. So were others for security reason: to prevent escapes. Inspections came before every move. I had to display all my belongings and I was thoroughly searched for forbidden objects: salt, sharp metal things, matches and dried food.

Section F consisted of 12 cells. They came in pairs like a duplex. I had a false sense of pleasantness when I first came because the weather was still mild in early December. I felt secure in case typhoons come. However, after I spent two winters and one summer there, I had different memories. It was hot like hell and cold like hell, too; or it seemed so because I was not fed enough. The cell was practically a concrete box of 7 meters long x 2.5 meters wide x 2.5 meters high with the wall and ceiling of more than 0.4 meter thick. It had only a very small window with iron bars like a window in a bird cage way up near the ceiling. In the summer, Ha Tay could reach over 100 degrees F; I had to sleep in sweat and naked with my pants covering my loins. In the winter, it could go down to 35 degrees F. I wore four pairs of clothes plus two thick blankets and I was still shivering. Captain T. later told me that the American POWs used to be in these cells. I shared their sufferings. It must have been worse for them in the summer because they weren't born in a tropical region as I did.

A few times I was escorted to the well by the kitchen for bathing, before an interrogation by some big shot, I guessed. I was cleaner that way but I felt embarrassed because of heavy guards around. Section F didn't have a well for itself. Every day I got hot water twice along with my meals. Each time I got about one liter, equal to 1.05 quart. Those two liters of water were for my daily need: drinking, cleaning and washing.

At meal time, I didn't drink until I finished eating then I carefully poured water onto my chopsticks and spoon to clean them while the dirty bowl was placed underneath. No water was wasted. I then cleaned the inside of the bowl with my fingers and drank that water instead of dumping it out. No food was wasted either.

For my bath, I saved water until I had about one liter. I would dip a tiny piece of cloth with my fingers into the water, then dab and rub it on my forehead before I went slowly around and downward. The sensation of water, however little, running down my skin gave me the feeling of cleanliness. Once my feet were washed, I poured the rest of the water over my head to wash my hair. I saved the best feeling for the last moment that way. I knew a cellmate who had his unique way of taking a shower. He made a few little holes at the bottom of an empty tin can, hung it above his head then he poured water in. I could see his ecstatic face every time he was under those shower-by-the-drops. The rest of us in the cell didn't imitate him. We respected his copyright. We didn't have his patience anyway.

I had my happy time if a rain shower happened during the day. The gate was always closed, but the door was open from 8:00 AM to 5:00 PM. I would go out bathing and washing my clothes in the rain. Fresh, cool water was good for my mental health. Other people did the same thing in the little area between the gate and the door. I think the American POWs might have done the same thing, too.

My first week of doing nothing in Section F, Ha Tay camp gave me a false sense of pleasantness and peacefulness. I was so naïve! I didn't know that the Communists prepared me for the drilling to come.

<4>

5- The Dungeon Game, Part Two: The Drilling

I knew the Communists considered me as "a dangerous war criminal" when they handcuffed me, secretly took me to the north and confined me in Section F of Ha Tay camp. I learned how "dangerous" I was in the 14 months of confinement. I experienced a world upside down during interrogation sessions. Getting an American education became "Being brainwashed in American Imperialism"; and Fighting against Communism became "Committing bloody crimes against the people." I am sure the notion of Right and Wrong was twisted in the mind of the American POWs, too. I admired them for surviving Communist interrogation tactics. I experienced these tactics myself.

The interrogation started after I was given a week of doing nothing. During that week, Captain T. brought us state-run newspaper every day for group reading one hour daily. That was all we had to do. Some of my older cellmates, like General Nhu, warned me of interrogation ahead when I exclaimed the pleasantness of being in Section F. He was in Viet Minh prison during the forties. He was a Vietnamese nationalist who fought against the French, but he opposed Viet Minh. He knew the Vietnamese Communists were under the disguise of Viet Minh as a national front to attract patriotic youth.

I began seeing Captain T. call, one person at a time, to go out with him. They all came back with a grim face. In their hands, they all had paper, a handle with a nibble, and an inkpot. They sat on the table in the patio that was used for eating to write; or they sat right at their sleeping space to write. They wrote in silence. They kept a distance from each other, partly because they didn't want others to see their writing; partly because others weren't working in the same unit with them. The Communists intentionally separated people working in the same unit to different cells. The superiors could still influence the writing of the subordinates or they all could agree on writing the same thing if they were in the same cell. The Communists didn't want that to happen. The Communists wanted reports that they could make comparisons and they could find out different details for their advantages. I was never in the same cell with my direct or indirect superior during my 14 months in confinement. My intelligence organization wasn't evacuated; the whole unit went into concentration camps together, from the top to the bottom.

During the time in Long Thanh camp (June 1975 to October 1976), I was told to write my personal history and my employment history more than ten times, each time the cadres demanded more details. Before leaving for the north, the last demand was "How can you help to consolidate the successful Revolution?" I was eager to share my knowledge of geography and my experience of studying abroad. I was thinking that my American education would be useful to the new regime, that I would soon have a job after re-education. I was so naïve!

I felt a splash of cold water into my face with the very first interrogator. He looked at me with angry eyes and threw my last writing on the table:

"Why are you playing game with the Revolution? We asked you to help consolidate our success and you wrote meaningless trash! Why didn't you write about your post-war strategy? How many agents did you order to become sleepers? Who are they? Where are they? What did your American advisor tell you about the American post-war scheme?"

The interrogator clearly gave me the notion that the Communists were afraid of the Trojan horse strategy. In 1954, the Communists left the Trojan horse in South Vietnam when they signed the Geneva Agreement with the French to divide Vietnam into two parts. Now they went after me to see if the Americans and my unit did something similar to their tactics.

The interrogator wore plain clothes. He was in his forties. I assumed he worked in the unit that took over my unit when he said he was at my desk. He smirked at me:

"You got two commendations in just three and a half years at work; and you were promoted just after three years. You must be very good at snooping on us, heh?"

I saw his remarks as a threatening tactic saying, "Don't lie to me." I answered him the best I could. He concluded his session in two hours. I believed he recorded it. He gave me paper, a wooden handle with a nibble and an ink pot.

"I give you a week to write what I ask you today. I expect better answers than what I heard. I don't want to reduce your daily ration, you hear?"

Another threatening tactic, but it was for real as I experienced it down the road.

I didn't hide anything from him or other interrogators. In the last minutes at work, I was ordered not to burn my work because there was the foolish hope that the Communists would stop the attack and agree to a peace settlement. Besides, I didn't have anything to cling on for hope like the American POWs did. My government was gone. The last President, General Minh, declared a total surrender. The ex-President, Mr. Thieu, deserted nine days before the end. I, myself, was sick of the incompetence and the corruption of Mr. Thieu's leading staff. I didn't blame the United States for leaving South Vietnam. I blamed Mr. Thieu and his staff (with me in it) for not making it worthy to be supported by the Americans. Why didn't the Americans abandon South Korea? Why didn't the Americans abandon West Germany? Those "Whys" have been the burning questions in my mind. I was taught by Confucianism: "*Blame thyself before blaming others.*"

The first interrogator and the others weren't satisfied with my answers. I was asked verbally and I was ordered to write over and over again in the following ten months.

Some of the questions were unheard of in Western governments, such as: "Who was the real leader in your unit?" and "What special privileges did you have?" The Communists asked me those questions because they thought the South Vietnam government operated on principles like them. They have the Communist Party structure which is hidden and parallel to the open structure. The real power is in the hand of the Party members in that open structure. A person might be a vice chairman in the open organizational chart, but he is the decision maker instead of the chairman if he is the Party secretary in that organization. The Party members also have special privileges that a non-Party official does not have. The President in a Communist country doesn't make decisions, the Party Secretary does.

The writing became very hard in the winter. I couldn't sit and write on the table in the patio. It was too cold and windy. So I set up my table on my sleeping space. I piled up all the clothes and blankets to make a stack. I smoothed out the top. Voila! That was my table. My fingers got stiff even inside the cell so I could only write about three pages a day at best. I also had to dip the nibble into the inkpot after every few words I wrote on the coarse, brownish paper…

I was especially drilled very hard on how many informers I had in Hanoi and how many spies I sent to Hanoi, too. I told the interrogators that I was working in the research department. I had nothing to do with espionage; but they didn't believe me.

"Liar! You wrote about your interrogation with the traitors." One interrogator pointed his finger at me with his teeth clenched.

"I was granted special permission to interview the defectors." I stressed the words "interview the defectors" to correct him. "My direct superior arranged the interviews with the head of the other department. You can ask him to verify."

I wasn't physically tortured at any time. I was just mentally tortured when the interrogators thought I was not telling the truth. During those grilling sessions, the interrogators slammed the table, stood up overpowering me, or ordered me to stand stiff to answer their questions, to identify this or that face. Back in the cell, my ration was reduced for days at a time. I wasn't given a fourth of the fist-sized boiled bun for breakfast on those particular days.

I had a few good days though. An army colonel came. He didn't act as an interrogator. He stood up to shake my hand and he offered me a cigarette before asking me questions. I was instantly and constantly on guard of his friendliness. He asked me about my college years in California. I was very tense at first because I thought he was probing me to see if I had any connections with CIA. He asked me to write, too. He came back several times asking me particularly about the school I attended, California State College at Fullerton (which became University in the seventies). He gave me cigarettes and candies for my answers. A few years later,

I happened to read an article on the state-run newspaper that a delegation of Hanoi University professors visited Cal State Fullerton. They were greeted by two CSUF professors, one of them with the name Cooper. I wondered if I had anything to do with it. I had told the Communist army colonel about two very active anti-war professors at CSUF at the time I was studying there. I had a few unpleasant encounters with Professor Cooper of Chemistry Department at the anti-war demonstrations on campus.

I wasn't taken to the highest level of interrogation: Hanoi Hilton. My direct superior, the Director of Intelligence Research (equivalent to a lieutenant colonel) and my indirect superior, the Chief of Central Intelligence Organization (equivalent to a one-star general) were taken there several times, I was told later.

The interrogation period seemed to end after ten months for me. During the next four following months, I was given plenty of paper and ink to write about my life, from childhood to my last working day. I wrote a 300 page account of my life. I seized the opportunity to tell the Communists about the free world I was in. Of course I had to mask it under the form of the confession like this:

"I was deceived by American imperialism when I stepped on board the Boeing 707 of Pan Am Airlines. It wasn't made of paper as the cadres claimed! It was a solid airplane with all the devilish advanced technologies that lured me deeper and deeper into its wings…" or

"I witnessed dirty capitalism at its worst when I visited the cement factory in Fontana, California. It was not a People's factory, of course; so the workers weren't allowed to volunteer working overtime for free. The Satanic factory owners disguised their exploitation by paying high wages to suck workers' labor. The workers all came to work in their own cars instead of walking or bicycling. Their saved energy will be exploited by the capitalists…"

I was taken back to Section A, Ha Tay camp at the end of February 1978. I was told that I now entered the stage of doing the manual task to transform myself. I was assigned to the brick-making group. I thought my interrogation ordeal was over until one day…

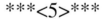

<5>

6- Down to the Bottom, Part One: Almost R.I.P

I came to my lowest point in life after I got out of Section F. A string of events combined with youthful reasoning led me to the drastic decision of ending my life.

I was put back to Section A, Ha Tay camp at the end of February 1978. The 14-month interrogation period in Section F was done, I thought, when I was assigned to the brick-making group in Ward 2. I was ready to put my past behind and looking forward to having no more trouble with it. Four months later trouble came back to me, big time.

In mid-1978, I received gift number one from my mother. I was allowed two gifts of 5 kilograms [1 kilogram=2.2 pounds] a year, one in June and one in December. The Communists still hid me and other political prisoners at Ha Tay camp from the outside world. They told us prisoners to use the mail box 15 NV[2] for correspondence. While in confinement, I had written to my fiancée telling her not to wait for me. I was both sad and happy to receive the next gift from my mother. Through my younger brother's handwriting, my mother told me to take care of myself so I could come back to see her. The message was clear: No more fiancée.

---

[2] *NV, I guessed, was the abbreviation for Noi Vu (Ministry of Interior). The Communist prison system belonged to the Ministry of Interior.*

A few days after I got the gift, cadre Nhi called me to the command post. He was a first lieutenant security police officer in liaison with Hanoi headquarters. He told me to report to him the following day for a meeting with someone from Hanoi. For the first time I was given some advance information about the interrogation. Looking at my concerned face, cadre Nhi smiled, "Just routine questions, don't worry."

The interrogator dressed in Communist formal attire for dignitaries. Cadre Nhi gave up his office for the meeting. I felt nervous. I sensed something wasn't right. The man even shook my hand as he entered the room. He bragged about the changing South under Communism, then suddenly he said:

"I have a proposal for you. You shouldn't refuse it." I could see he was trying to smile.

"Cadre, I can't say Yes or No until you tell me what it is." I felt a chill spreading down my spine.

"We will release you and make arrangement for you to escape to America." He lowered his voice, "with one condition, you must work for us." He looked at me intensely.

The man had opened up his card, just as I predicted. I had heard rumors about a few high ranking officials who were questionably released early. The rumors were true then.

I had anticipated this scenario, so I made up my mind about it. I expected to see his anger as I said:

"Cadre, I promise myself that I would never be involved in intelligence again. I am sorry. I just want to be a normal person from now on."

"You dare to refuse Revolutionary's request?" He stood up abruptly and stared at me.

"I am sorry. I don't deserve to receive that honor." I looked back at him and shook my head. I played for broke. I was at the bottom of the well. I had nothing to lose. In a bitter voice, I explained my refusal:

"If this Revolutionary's request was offered to me when I first stepped into re-education camp, I would've accepted it. Too late now, cadre. I know who I am after being handcuffed and brought here."

Seeing the determination on my face, the man backed down. He gave me his fountain pen and a piece of paper from his brown leather portfolio case:

"Draw me the secret chart of your Intelligence Research Department." He coaxed me.

"Cadre, I don't know about it. I had told other cadres that we didn't have the power play like the Communist Party does."

"Liar! Thieu[3] had his party. You must've played a role in it. You got hired right after you came back from America. Don't play the innocence game with me!" He raised his voice.

"Cadre, I don't know what else to say. Nobody ever asked me to join Mr. Thieu's party. I had no

---

[3] *Mr. Thieu was the President of South Vietnam, 1967-1975.*

knowledge of his party members in my department." I gently pushed the piece of paper back to him.

The man looked at me and clenched his teeth. I looked back defiantly. The game of nerves was escalating. I wasn't afraid of his interrogation because I had experienced it before. He thought he would play upper hand with his attire. I was impressed by it but I wasn't humiliated. The man softened his look:

"I am giving you my last offer to work for the Revolutionary: Spy on your direct boss, NKT for us. I'll make arrangement for you to be with NKT at Hanoi Hilton."

"No, thank you, cadre. I'm not good at doing that with anyone; and I can't turn myself against my boss." I kept calm at his move. I even gave him a soft smile, *"The flame for passions inside me has gone; no longer I care about earthly things."* I recited a famous verse from the 18th century poet that all Vietnamese should know.

He lost his patience at my answer. He shoved his chair back noisily and stood up, pointing his finger at me:

"You definitely are a CIA agent! I will unmask you! Just wait and see!" He stomped out of cadre Nhi's office.

My heart sank at his accusation and his threat. No interrogators said those things to me before. I felt so tired of this game of nerves. In a flash, I made up my mind to prove that I wasn't working for CIA, once and for all. I came back to the ward with a smile on my face. I didn't want to show my intention to anyone. I secretly felt a rush of joy because I was about to go on the voyage that no one else could go with me. I would be free at last. I no longer had any reasons to cling on to this life in prison.

I came back to the ward while my brick-making group was still at work. I enjoyed the time being alone by myself. I had time to write to my mother the last letter with the paper and pen she sent. Sadness came back to me for leaving her, but I also wrote that I was happy to see my father soon. I had been in prison four months when my father died of cancer in October 1975.

As the prison bell from the command post struck nine, I got ready for my departure. I decided that I should have a full stomach to go on my voyage. I set up my mosquito net as usual and sat inside. I opened my mother's gift, took out all the food and ate it, no need for saving any more. Once done with eating, I sorted out the medicine my mother sent me. I took 20 pills of antibiotics, 20 pills for diarrhea, 40 pills of aspirin, and all of the vitamin pills. The more the better, I thought. I swallowed the last gulp of water and lay down. I put the letter for my mother on my chest, folded my arms and whispered "I am sorry, Mother." Tears ran down from the corners of my eyes but nobody could see them because the light was turned off.

FAREWELL, this miserable upside down world…

<6>

7- Down to the Bottom, Part Two: The Silver Lining

"Every cloud has a silver lining." Really?

I didn't think so when I felt so desperate that I committed suicide and failed in June 1978. I expected more bad things followed; but good things unexpectedly happened. The years of going downward seemed to reach the lowest point for me; I was about to go upward, however slowly…

My failed suicide attempt made the breaking news in the ward the morning after. I had told my neighbor not to say anything to anybody when I asked him for help, and he did otherwise. I woke up in a half-conscious state during the night after a few very bad throw-ups. I was a smelly mess in my mosquito net. I couldn't get up myself; I was too weak. I had to wait until I could see the morning light through the iron bars then I tapped my neighbor on the right and whispered:

"Brother Lam, please help me. I tried to kill myself but couldn't. I threw up all over."

"What did you do?" Lam got up like a spring.

He reached his hand through his mosquito net and mine to touch me. He found the mess. He didn't say anything further.

"I took all the medicines my mother sent me. I couldn't die." I broke down in tears quietly.

I called Lam my brother because a friendship had grown since I was back from Section F four months earlier. He was 12 years older than me.

As I regained consciousness, I told brother Lam that I was cornered by the last interrogator. I didn't go into details. Somehow, the story came back to me later that I tried to kill myself because my fiancée left me. Good, I didn't protest the rumor. I didn't want to explain further sensitive details to anyone.

Anyone but cadre Nhi, the liaison officer who arranged the last interrogation for the man from Hanoi with me. I didn't expect sympathy from cadre Nhi. He called me up to his office two days later. As soon as I sat down opposite him, he took out a letter from his desk drawer. It was tainted and crumbled. He showed it to me with his angry eyes and a harsh tone:

"Why did you do this?"

I suddenly realized that was the letter I wrote to my mother. I totally forgot about it. I guessed brother Lam had to give it to the warden as evidence when he reported the incident. Well, so much for denial then. I had to tell cadre Nhi in details about the interrogation. He listened to me without interruption. When I finished talking, he asked me:

"Will you try to kill yourself again?"

"Yes, and I **will not** fail next time." I said as a matter of fact.

"You fool!" He exploded. "Don't you dare do it again! I confiscate this letter to report to my comrade superior in Hanoi. I'm not going to discipline you. I will suggest disciplinary action for the comrade who talked to you. He went too far. I told him not to push you."

I broke into tears right there. I had always tried to keep my feelings in check in front of my enemy. Somehow I didn't see cadre Nhi as an enemy anymore. He paused a moment, then said with a softer voice,

"You still have a life in front of you. We won't keep you here forever." He gave me some paper.

"You write your self-criticism for me. And I want you to include your promise that you **will not** do this foolish thing again. Clear?"

I was given a week free of labor work. I had time to think about why I couldn't die. Brother Lam had laughed at me when I told him I wanted to be a ghost with full stomach instead of a starved ghost. He said, "Lucky you, the food diluted the effect of the medicines." He also said that the medicines didn't kill me because they were busy fighting between themselves. I took too many kinds of medicines, anti-biotic, aspirin, diarrhea pills and especially the vitamins. He teased me that next time, if I wanted to do it again, just take only one kind of medicine; and quinine (for malaria) would be the best.

"You aren't a big person, just ten pills of quinine would do the job", he patted my back.

I came back to work in the brick-making group under watchful eyes of everybody in the group. Even the cadre in charge of the brick-making group seemed friendlier.

The silver lining was that I no longer had to do full time labor. Cadre Nhi started giving me books to translate off and on.

I had mixed emotions when I was handed the first book. It was about American and Russian strategies in the cold war. Just to see the cover in English was enough to bring tears into my eyes. I thought I would never see anything from the free world again. I held the book in my hand and yet I was a world apart from it. I did the translation with enthusiasm because it was my chance to refresh my English and my knowledge. Some people silently saw me as a traitor and kept a distance from me. They saw my translation as giving knowledge to the enemy, thus I became a collaborator. I thought otherwise. I felt that God was giving me my chance to show the Vietnamese Communists how America was far better than their Soviet Union and China. Later, after the war between China and Viet Nam broke out in 1979, I was given books on Chinese strategies written by American Think Tank, too. It was really a strange twist: I was dealing with intelligence research again.

Somebody else thought I chose to do translation to avoid manual labor, to avoid being in the heat and the cold with the brick-making group. Well, I couldn't please everyone, could I? My mother told me to take care of myself. Cadre Nhi told me to take it easy because he knew I didn't get much from the gifts that were sent by my mother. I believed he was helping me to get extra food when he introduced a cadre from the People's Army newspaper. That cadre needed a translation for the book "*The Fall of Saigon*" by David Butler. He gave me sugar, cakes, tea, and cigarettes every two weeks he came to get my translation. Later on, I saw the translation of the book on the People's Army newspaper all right, with a colonel's name as the translator. No wonder he was generous to me.

My best memory about translation was on a book written about Boat People in 1982. Boat People became known to the world in 1978 after a wave of Communist campaigns to change the money system and to destroy capitalist commercialism in South Vietnam. I didn't really know why I was given the book for translation because it was full of horrible tales against Communism. It was my best chance to attack Communism without being punished.

I still remember the moment that things started looking up for us. After a family visit, my friend discreetly asked me to translate something. He showed me a clipped article in English from a Bangkok newspaper. It said that Hanoi probed the U.S. about political prisoners when a Hanoi delegation visited Thailand in 1979. It was cleverly folded and inserted in between the wrappings of a Dove soap bar. We interpreted Dove as a symbol of flying and hope. How thoughtful of my friend's wife!

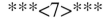

<7>

8- Message Understood

There are instances in life that a song could carry a special meaning. I experienced two of such songs. The first one was "White Christmas" as a message for the American evacuation out of South Vietnam on April 29, 1975. The second one happened while I was in Communist concentration camps. The song was the SOS message to the free world.

After the fall of Saigon in April 1975, there were roughly twenty five thousand South Vietnamese army officers and government officials being transported secretly to the North in 1976 for "re-education." We prisoners were put in concentration camps in the provinces around Hanoi and along the border with China. The Vietnamese communists wanted to hide the political prisoners and to make sure that no one would be able to escape. I was among the prisoners in Ha Tay camp, 30 miles southwest of Hanoi. I thought that was it: the end of my freedom for the rest of my life.

In February 1979, the Communist China's army crossed the border to attack Communist Vietnam. China's intention was to teach Vietnam a lesson for toppling the Pol Pot regime, China's ally in Kampuchea (formerly known as Cambodia). Sensing the attack was inevitable, in January 1979 the Vietnamese Communists hurriedly moved the political prisoners away from the border with China. Ha Tay camp doubled its capacity from one thousand to more than two thousand inmates. The width of my sleeping space was reduced from a full mat (about a yard) to half mat. Nobody was able to sleep on his back. The ration was less; the stench was more. The prison condition was getting worse and desperate until one day around September that year…

We, the prisoners, heard the screaming sound of the pigs being killed early one morning. At first, I thought it came from the cadres' living quarter. We all woke up and listened intensely as someone making a bet that it was from the prison kitchen. I realized then the screams were indeed from the prison kitchen, and more than one pig was being killed. What was going on? Then came the footsteps of the guard and the rattling sounds of the padlocks being opened and long iron bars being pulled to open the gate of the section and the door of the ward. The warden rushed in, yelling:

"Everybody, get up! You have thirty minutes to get ready. All team leaders have five minutes to report to the command post."

It was definitely not the usual daily order.

The team leaders came back shortly after. Everybody was waiting, chatting, and speculating noisily. Moving to another camp? Shuffling time? Inspection time? Someone being disciplined? All the speculations couldn't explain the screams of the pigs, though. I heard my team leader requested with a shaking voice:

"Half of you need to roll up your mat and take your belongings away, please. You, You, and You…do it."

I was pointed at. I had to roll up my mat, and took it with my two handbags to go hide them outside, in the back of the ward. The other half were told to clean and spread their full mats, and tidy their belongings, then put them at the top of the mat. That didn't explain our curiosity about the screams of the pigs in any way.

At 7:00 AM, one hour before the usual working time, everybody was ordered to go out with the guards except a few was chosen from each ward to report to the command post. The chosen ones were picked by the team cadre. I wasn't chosen and I realized from the way he picked that I wasn't trusted. One team after another was led by the guards to leave the prison. They didn't take us prisoners to our normal worksites which were around the cadres' living quarter or along the road into the camp. Instead, they took us all to the backside of the camp until we got into the hillside with bushes that blocked our view of the camp. Since no team cadres went with us, the guards told us that there was no work,

"Just be quiet and wait."
Hmm, very unusual, I thought.

We waited and waited past noon time. Everybody was starving under the hot sun. The guards were hungry and even upset. Finally we heard the sound of the prison bell to call us back after a day's work. The guards told us to hurry, and they didn't care if we were noisy on the way back. Once inside the prison, I noticed the wardens were in their neat uniforms. They came to receive their teams. We were told to come back to the ward, have lunch and take the rest of the day off. Wow! Very unusual again.

The first thing struck me as I went into the ward was the nice smell of pork and hot rice. How could it be? It wasn't a Communist holiday, and it certainly wasn't Lunar New Year yet. And here I was with a bowl of real vegetable soup, two finger-sized pieces of pork in it, and a bowl of white rice. I was happy! My daily meal was a bowl of ocean soup (all water with a few vegetable leaves, no meat) and a bowl of corn, or cassava, or yam mixed with a few grains of rice that I could easily single out.

During my happy meal, I learned that a group of international visitors came to the camp. Certainly they were more or less pro-communist but the camp management team didn't take any chance to expose the real conditions of the prison. And now that explained the screams of the pigs! The visitors would go back to the outside word and attest that we were treated decently.

The chosen ones to stay in the camp were ordered not to speak English, and if they were asked by the visitors, they had to speak through an interpreter with the following guidelines:

> ***They do not know English***
> ***They are re-educationees, not prisoners***
> ***They are treated nicely***

They are not forced to do hard labor.

After that first visit which caught us prisoners by surprise, we were able to guess when we would have international visitors coming: The screaming sound of the pigs, the re-arrangement of mats and the go-into-hiding game until the visitors left the camp.

As the visits became more frequent, the wardens selected a dozen prisoners who could play music to entertain the visitors. Their other purpose was to show the outside world that we prisoners were given time to enjoy ourselves as we had a musical band of our own. Truthfully, the band existed only on the days that the international visitors came.

At the beginning, the band was ordered to play communist music only. There weren't many songs available, and perhaps the cadres and the guards got bored with their own music so they let the band play other kinds of music. The cadres and the guards came to love the music from The Shadows and The Ventures, etc… I wasn't in the band, but I was sleeping next to the member who played mandolin in the band. And I was shared a secret late one night.

By 1981, Hanoi had allowed selected visitors from the free world to visit the camps. It was a visit by an international human rights group that we prisoners found a way to send the SOS message to them, and the camp cadres were unaware of it. After a tour around the camp, the visitors were guided to the "recreational room" in the middle of the camp for a briefing. The chief warden told them that there were no prisoners here, only re-educationees waiting to be returned to their families once they were deemed "having good progress." The band was told to play with enthusiasm after the briefing as proof of the warden's words. So, as usual, the band started with some Vietnamese communist songs, then playing the instrumental version of some Cuban, Chinese and Russian songs.

As the visitors were about to leave, the group played a song by The Shadows. That caught the attention of the visitors. Then the band started playing the song from the movie "*The Bridge Over The River Kwai*".[4] The smiles on the faces of the visitors faded away quickly. The band members didn't dare to look up for long because tears were swelling in their eyes. They pretended to be concentrating on playing the song. They heard a rather loud THANK YOU as the visitors were leaving. When the last footsteps were at the door, my mandolin friend and a few glanced up. They caught a slight nod from the last visitor out: **MESSAGE UNDERSTOOD**

A week later, the musical band was called to report to the command post. Members of the band were questioned intensely by furious cadres. The cadres found out the meaning of "*The Bridge Over The River Kwai*" through an informer. The band members were disciplined. They were

---

[4] *"The Bridge Over The River Kwai" was an Oscar-winning movie in 1957. It was about American and British POWs (Prisoners of War) during World War II in Burma. Its theme song was very well-known in the '60s.*

put in confinement for a week with one meal a day. The band leader was punished double, two weeks.

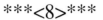

9- Breaking up An Antenna

In January 1979, I had new fellow prisoners at Ha Tay concentration camp, 30 miles southwest of Hanoi. They were middle ranking military officers from South Vietnam army. They were brought from the south to the provinces along the border of Vietnam and China in 1976, and now they were transferred down to Ha Tay. They were moved because the war between Communist China and Communist Viet Nam was inevitable at the border between the two countries. China had threatened "to teach Vietnam a lesson" since Vietnam toppled Pol Pot regime, China's best ally, in Kampuchea (formerly known as Cambodia) near the end of 1978.

The atmosphere in the prison suddenly became tenser. I had less space for sleeping. I felt the meal was less, too. Everything took longer to do: going out and in for roll call, going to the toilet, going to the well for bathing and washing clothes. The most noticeable tension was the attitude of these army officers. They openly said that they, the newcomers, were not afraid of the wardens and the cadres. They made comments that the old timer prisoners like me were chicken, too tame. That was true. Ha Tay camp had been a place for South Vietnam government officials and police force. I didn't face death on the battle fields like most of the military officers; therefore, I wasn't as daring as they were.

They also lamented that they became "suffocated" in Ha Tay camp. Earlier, they were under the Communist army's management which was more relaxed. They were not locked behind doors at night because they were in the deep jungle. Ha Tay camp was run by Communist security police force with a brick wall about one foot thick. I was locked behind doors at night because the camp was surrounded by villages in a rural area.

The brick-making group I was in had new faces. Tension began. They slowed down production of every team in the group. The transport team took more time to bring in the clay from the field. The clay team was slower in feeding the clay to the cutting machine. The drying team was dragging raw bricks to the yard for drying under the sun. These new men ignored the cadres' yelling to speed things up. They worked, but they just couldn't work fast because of hunger and fatigue as they replied to the cadres. To make things worse, they broke many prison rules. They secretly brought wood into the ward to cook after being locked up. They secretly had makeshift knives. They gathered into small groups at night to have tea and smoke and discuss politics openly. They made me old timer prisoner on edge because the wardens would soon know about their violations. The command post would certainly make life miserable for me and others once they got word of the violations.

Six nights a week, we prisoners had to gather in groups to listen to the state-run newspaper read by team leaders before discussions on daily matters. Violations by the newcomers were pointed out and warned by team leaders. Instructions to deal with violations were surely coming from the command post. Self-criticism and self-correction were encouraged. The newcomers didn't care a bit. They swore and cursed even more.

Sure enough, on the third Sunday after the newcomers came, the command post ordered a thorough inspection of the wards. We prisoners were ordered out of the ward on the double and were told to sit still on the ground. One by one we were escorted back inside to take our mat and our belongings out. There were about a hundred prisoners in each ward. We were told to display everything we had on our mats. What wasn't allowed was confiscated. The guards had their rifles ready to shoot. The newcomers had the first taste of prison rules that were nothing new to us old timers. That inspection lasted past lunch time. The command post didn't care a bit. The cadres, the wardens and the guards took turns to go to lunch. The prisoners had to stay put on the ground outside the ward until the last one was inspected. Whew!

Swearing, cursing and blaming were loud after the inspection. We were aware that there were informers among us prisoners. The group leaders and the team leaders were the obvious informers as they had contacts with the wardens and the cadres every day. We didn't share our secrets with them. We were puzzled when the cadres and wardens picked out exactly someone's violation like a makeshift knife, a little jar of salt, or a box of matches. Those items were on the prison's black list for escape survival. The newcomers were very upset when they realized that they were reported by a secret informer. Who could that person be? They decided to find out. One night, a week later…

As usual, the bell from the command post struck three times at 9:00 PM to give prisoners one hour to go to sleep. The lights went out at 10:00 PM to save fuel used by the generator. Suddenly, I heard noises, clashes and screams in the middle of the ward:

"Oh My God! People hit me! Help! Help me!" cried a voice.

"Report to warden, someone is being beaten in Ward number 8! Report to warden, someone is being beaten in Ward number 8!" shouted the ward leader through the iron bars of a window.

The commotion continued. Thumping, hitting and screaming sounded loudly in the dark. When the footsteps of the guards and the warden came near, the commotion suddenly stopped. Only the screaming and crying of the victim were heard. Flash light beams scanned crisscrossed the ward through the iron bars, along with the warden's yelling:

"Who is beaten? Ward leader, bring him to the door!"

"Report to warden, the beaten one is D." answered the ward leader.

"Bring him to the door! Who beat him?"

"Report to warden, we don't know. We were sleeping. It was dark. D. was covered with a blanket then beaten by a few. We don't know who who…"

The guards and the warden of Ward number 8 waited more than five minutes for the lights to come back on before they unlocked the door, pulled the steel bar across the door and stepped in. They saw D. lying on the blanket with a bloody nose and bruises on his face and his bare upper torso. Only the ward leader was out talking to the warden and the guards. The rest of the prisoners were sitting inside their mosquito nets, looking out quietly and innocently. The warden and the guards, with their fiery eyes, walked back and forth the entire ward looking for clues. None. There was nothing they could do at the moment. The warden ordered D. to be carried to the sick room near the prison kitchen. When the ward leader came back, the door was locked and the lights went out again. I could hear whispers and giggles but all the excitement turned silent when I heard very faint footsteps outside.

The newcomers had made the deduction that D. was the secret antenna (prison slang for informer). He was a major in the South Vietnam Police Force. He had enough knowledge of mechanics and electricity to volunteer to be a handyman for the cadres. By 1979, a great deal of American appliances from South Vietnam was brought to the North. The cadres didn't know how to fix it if something went wrong. It wasn't unusual to see D. go to the cadres' living quarter to fix things and come back with tales about cadres. He seemed harmless until the last inspection. He joined the newcomers for tea at night and made jokes about the cadres as his contribution. A good camouflaged antenna he was!

Of course the whole Ward number 8 was punished for the beating. Nobody confessed. The cadres at the command post couldn't find the culprits although they made heavy threats. The punishment was "no going out to the well for bathing and washing clothes in four consecutive Sundays." I had to manage my bathing and washing on weekdays before or after work. The last very least bit of freedom was taken away, just like that.

D. didn't come back to Ward number 8. He was transferred to another ward. The news about the incident spread among prisoners. D. seemed to behave better from then on.

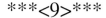

<9>

10-   Family Visits

I never thought how a family visit could be so memorable until I was in Communist concentration camps. I had seen the joy and the agony of family visits of my fellow prisoners; and how those visits affected everybody, including the cadres and the wardens in the camp.

For the first four years, June 1975 to around October 1979, the Communists didn't allow family visits. They only allowed gifts, twice a year, starting at the end of 1976 when they secured us prisoners in North Vietnam. They hid us from the outside world. They were afraid of the American post-war strategy, something like the Trojan horse. They drilled me and drilled me about it while they put me in confinement for 14 months.

The first family visits were allowed in October 1979. The Communists had yielded to the international outcry for human rights as Boat People reached the free world. Tales of horrible living conditions were told. The other reason was the American embargo combined with the Communist unrealistic economic measures had made the Vietnamese economy at its worst. The Communists had to lift the bamboo curtain to survive. The whole nation was eating cassava, potatoes and yam mixed with rice. In prison, I witnessed deaths from starvation and diseases every week. Some of the deaths were right next to me.

The camp authority set the first family visit at 15 minutes. The cadres wanted to show their control as victors. They even required a good labor record for a family visit. The wives of the prisoners were angry and frustrated. They came from the south, a thousand miles away, on a trip by train of three days and three nights to Hanoi; then they had to take a local bus to the town near the camp. From the town, they walked 2-3 miles on dirt roads to the camp with their belongings. All of that hard work and time earned only 15 minutes of seeing their loved ones.

The wives were outraged at the time limit. They petitioned. They protested. They begged the camp authority to change the time limit to no avail. What to do? They staged a protest in front of the Ministry of Interior in Hanoi. Since some of them had Communist relatives, their voices were heard. The camp authority reluctantly changed the rule for visiting to overnight stay. Things started to change for the better. A long drought seemed to come to an end.

My brick-making group had to work double time to make bricks for the construction group to build a reception building. We didn't mind. We did it in three months, just in time for the Lunar New Year visits. Those family visits just worked wonders.

The South Vietnamese people long have the tradition of giving the authorities something before they submit their request. It is called "*money goes first is wise money.*" Especially on the occasion of the Lunar New

Year, that tradition is a must, and no one would refuse it to avoid bad luck the whole year. The prisoners' wives didn't dare to give the camp authority anything big at first, just a pack of Western cigarettes for the cadres and some Western soap bars for his family. It made a huge impression on the cadres and the wardens because most of them never experienced the taste and the feel of those things. Tylenol and Aspirin became wonder drugs, followed by antibiotic medicines.

In Ha Tay camp, there were many generals and colonels who let their families evacuate first; then chaos spread so fast at the end that these generals and colonels were left behind and went into concentration camps. When the Communists allowed gifts from abroad in the early eighties, these generals and colonels reconnected with their families, and gifts poured into the camp through visits by their relatives. The camp authority got even more surprises. The cadres and the wardens began tasting butter, chocolate, whisky, shampoo, and much more. The rule for visiting became more relaxed, from one night to two or three, from one visit every six months to one visit every three months.

I was one of the orphans in the camp. Orphan was prison slang for a person who didn't have family visits for some reasons. In my case, my fiancée broke up with me and my mother was too poor to make a trip north. I got gifts only from my mother. I didn't feel left out by those family visits though. I was always happy to see others go out to the visitors' building. When they came back, they always gave me something and there always was a little party once we were locked inside at night. The orphans like me would be busy cooking hot snacks and boiling water for tea and coffee for everyone in the ward. Yes, I said cooking because kerosene was allowed and kerosene burners were skillfully made by some prisoners out of the tin cans. These impromptu parties soon had music as musical instruments were allowed. The ward became alive at night, no more atmosphere of dreaded silence with each person lying or sitting in his own mosquito net.

I never thought I would be doing "bombing missions" in prison, but I did as I transported raw clay from the field outside the prison to my brick-making team inside. A bomb was the prison slang for an illegal letter that a prisoner could sneak out of prison. I was scared stiff on the first mission for fear of being caught. The more I did, the braver I was and I felt I made a good contribution to my fellow prisoners. A kind of silver lining was found in bad circumstances.

As the rules of family visits were relaxed, so were the rules of escorting prisoners to get clay for the brick-making team. The guard might follow me and my two companions with the oxcart once in the morning and once in the afternoon. For the best part of the day, he would hang around the visitors' building where there were female cadres to chat with (and the guard certainly would get something from the visiting wives, too). We prisoners quickly took advantage of the changing situation. We set up a hidden mail box along the route. We described it to the person who was about to have his family visit so he could relay the information to his wife. On the way out to get clay, we hid all the bombs (prison slang for forbidden letters) somewhere in the oxcart and dropped in the mail box. The wives then got those "bombs" on the way out after the visit. After we did the first few missions, the wives got the hang of it so they dropped incoming letters before they came in. We now could read what was going on in the open society. Of course the bombing missions were highly secretive to avoid being reported by antennas (prison slang for informers); we did it only when we felt the risk was minimal.

The family visits and the hidden letters sometimes brought bad news: News of a wife who left all her children to the prisoner's parents so she could get married to a cadre, or news of the children who were sent on a boat out to the sea to seek freedom and never heard from them again…

The good news prevailed though. The prison's atmosphere became more pleasant, more joyful after the family visits started. We became alive, especially in the early morning. If we talked mostly about food during the years 1975-1979 and we were too weak to get "woody" in the morning, we now began talking about something else after family visits. Here are a few examples:

1) My fellow prisoner came back to the ward after his family visit. He got all the things he wanted but he didn't seem happy. I asked him the reason.

"My wife got robbed," said he, "and worse. The robber undressed her and made love to her." He showed me his fist and he clenched his teeth.

"Did your wife report to the police? Was he caught?" I was concerned.

"She couldn't. She said she did not dare to do that." He sighed.

"Why? Why?" I was angry myself.

"Because the robber was ME." He started laughing.

2) After the family visit, one day I noticed my neighbor had a shoe brush, the kind with no handle and the bristle was very fine. It fitted into one's hand nicely for doing the brushing, but he wasn't wearing shoes, neither were I and the rest of the prisoners. I was curious, so I asked him and he ignored me. I asked another fellow prisoner and I got a hit on my head with his knuckle:

"Highly-talented young man, don't you know? I guess you don't because you're not married yet. Ha.Ha.Ha…SShhh, find a way to watch him before he goes to sleep, OK?"

It took me a few nights before I noticed my neighbor was gently rubbing his palm back and forth on the bristle of the shoe brush in the dark. I thought it was weird. I told my fellow prisoner of my finding. Again, I got another hit on my head with his knuckle: "Dummy! You'll know it when you get married. I'm not going to tell you. It's a man's thing." And he shoved me away.

 He was right. I didn't understand it until I got married…

3) This last story came from Section F, where the Communists kept 23 generals from South Vietnam army. In a relative's visit, a general got the letter from his wife. The wife begged for his forgiveness as she was about to let their three daughters get married. Two daughters married in the United States and one in France. The general gave them his blessings and asked them to let him know how their marriages went along. He emphasized that they couldn't say much because the cadres read the mail.

A year later, he got the first report from his wife, "Our daughter in California with me sent you only one word: Marlborough King. I don't understand. Do you?" The general gently rubbed his hands together, "*Marlborough King Size*, Hhmm…Not bad."

The following month, he got another letter from his wife, "Our daughter in New York sent you the word Nescafé. What does that mean?" The general grinned, "Ah! *Good to the last drop*, how nice!"

Then came the word from their daughter in France. The general's wife was even more confused as it said: Air France. The general stroke his beard, "Wow! *Flights take off every half hour!*" And he was so happy…

(If I remember correctly, the general used the quotes from the commercials for those three products during 1960s, with pun intended)

<10>

11-   Was It Love?

The place was Nam Ha camp, about 50 miles south of Hanoi, North Vietnam. It was mid-1984. My shift ended at 2: 00 PM. I was washing myself when the kitchen group leader came to me:

"Ly, report to cadre An. She asked for you." He said with a sly smile and shrugged his shoulders.

I smelled trouble.

Cadre An (An means Peace in Vietnamese) was the warehouse keeper. She came temporarily to take charge of the prison kitchen while the kitchen cadre, Lieutenant Do, went on another duty for two months in Saigon and the South. I had seen cadre An before at the warehouse outside the prison wall. My fellow prisoners and I saw her weekly to get supplies for the kitchen. She was in her late twenties, not bad looking for a security police officer. She was still single. She had always kept a distance from us prisoners because she knew she was one of the very few female cadres in the camp. She was well aware that we longed to see a feminine figure after almost ten years in prison.

I was transferred to Nam Ha camp in 1983. My new labor duty was to work in the prison kitchen. To cook for a camp of more than 1200 prisoners was hard labor. The brighter side of it was better ration and no worries of hot or cold weather. Best of all was the privilege of bathing and washing clothes. The kitchen had its own well.

As I reported to her, cadre An stood up:

"Ly, I want to learn English. I want you to teach me like you teach comrade Do."

I noticed her soft voice and she called me by my name, not blank "mister". She also showed her manner as a student all right, but her direct approach made me feel uneasy. I didn't anticipate this kind of trouble. Sensing my hesitation, cadre An explained:

"The command post knows comrade Do is learning English from you. It's OK."

"Well, it's not OK to me because you are a lady cadre." I tried to get off the hook.

"Comrade Do spoke highly of you." She smiled. "And he said you wouldn't hate me. Would you?" She was direct again. Somehow I liked that.

"Cadre, it's the other way around. I thought you hated me." I smiled back.

"No, I was just keeping a safe distance from you and others. Now I feel safer knowing you." She was using female tactics to get things her way and did it well:

"Teacher, I want to learn English from you. I know you studied in America." She looked at me with admiration (or I thought so).

She was charming me with her dimples. I began to see her pretty although she was wearing a communist police uniform.

Learning English had become an "in" thing lately. The tide seemed to turn around in 1979. In February that year, China taught Vietnam a lesson with the war at the border between the two countries. China became "enemy number one." The once-declared "unbreakable friendship" with China was broken. People in North Vietnam suddenly opened their eyes to a new reality.

The anti-American sentiment was fading away. The state propaganda machine actually promoted a better relation with the US on state-run radio and newspaper every day. International groups were welcomed at concentration camps starting at the end of 1979. Cadres began to see the need of knowing English. They looked into prisoners' files to find out who could teach them. Learning English was not prohibited any more. Cadre Do became my student not long after I was ordered to report to him. Yes, he called himself "student" and me, his "teacher." Cadre An became my second student, a pretty one.

I faced hostile reaction from my fellow prisoners when I started teaching English to cadres. Some kept a distance from me because they thought I became an antenna (prison slang for informer). Some saw me as a traitor because I crossed the line to befriend with enemies. Putting the pros and cons on the scale, I decided the pros outweighed the cons. I had to do my small part in erasing the anti-American sentiment among cadres. Silently, I wanted to show the cadres "*Who is triumphant over whom*?" (That was the Communists' bragging remark when they won the war in 1975)

The kitchen worked seven days a week. Cadre An was there seven days a week. My shift was from 6:00 AM to 2:00 PM then my teaching was after 4:00 PM. The lesson was usually an hour with cadre Do. Somehow it lasted more than an hour with cadre An. The more I saw her, the prettier she was. I felt the feeling was mutual as I noticed she waited at the door for me. She was using the room made for cadre Do in a corner of the kitchen. I always made sure the door was at least half open while I was teaching her. I had to play it safe, for me and for her. I was certain that she and I were surrounded by informers. She might even have a secret follower watching over us, too.

On the fourth week of learning, while listening to me, cadre An suddenly said,

> "I know your fiancée left you." She looked straight into my eyes, tenderly.

I was caught off guard. I looked at her then turned my eyes away to avoid her look. She opened up my wound at the same time she opened herself.

> -"I am so sorry." She said. Her left hand touched my right hand holding the pen.

I could feel the warmth from her hand passing through my hand. I could hear her heartbeat through her touch, too. I was silent. Mixed feelings were all over me. I had kept my broken heart feelings pretty well to myself until now. She must have asked my group leader or he offered the news as he was the only one I talked about it. Anyway, it showed she cared. "What is going on from here?" I asked myself. I stood up to leave. She held my hand again, firmly.

"Teacher Ly, please don't leave." Her voice was emotional.

I stood still at the edge of the desk, trying to compose myself. She was the cadre and I was the prisoner. I didn't want to mess around with reality. She and I would be in big trouble with the command post if we started any kind of relationship. Besides, I would be a laughing stock to my fellow prisoners for being sucked into this foolish adventure. "*A pretty enemy is still an enemy.*" I was warned as they saw me teaching cadre An.

I calmed down. Her hand was still holding my hand. I sat down at the same time pulling my hand away from hers. I took courage to give her a stern look:

"Cadre, let's not waste our time."

She gave me a yielding glance then looked back to her notebook. I guessed my emphasis on the word "cadre" was enough to show her the wall between her and me.

The lessons continued. In the days followed, I noticed she tied her hair up high to make a pony tail while she was with me. During the day, her long hair was down to her shoulders. I couldn't help looking at her marble round neck. I thought she intentionally turned her head around once in a while so I could see her nape, just like she knew my weakness! The game was on, no doubt about it. I held my ground firmly though. Helping me to hold my ground was my group leader. He usually stayed late to report inventory and his plan for the following day to her. Rescuing me from temptations was the guard. At 6:00 PM, he escorted me and the group leader back to the ward and locked the door behind us.

Two weeks before cadre Do returned, cadre An told me about the rumors that America wanted to take the political prisoners. The cadres from Hanoi told her that my fellow prisoners and I have become their "strategic reserves".

"So?" I pretended not to be impressed.

"So I hope you will be released and go to America soon. I do." I felt her voice was genuinely sweet and honest.

Her words were music to my ears, but I had to be very cautious.

"Thank you. I don't know. I doubt it." said I.

"Teacher Ly, I've been thinking about you." She looked at me tenderly.

In a quick move, she grabbed my hands and brought them to her face. She turned so her lips were brushing my hands. Her soft lips and her hot breath melted my heart.

"Cadre, Thank you again. You and cadre Do have been very nice." I heard myself saying.

I tried to look at her calmly and change the course of conversation. She let go of my hands and looked hurt. Oh well…

I continued teaching her but I kept my distance. She knew I tried to avoid talking about affection and relationship. She played it cool herself by concentrating on her study. On her last day with the prison kitchen, she was very amiable to everyone. At the end of that day, just her and me, she gave me a handshake that quickly became a peck on my cheek before she hurried off. That was my sweetest day in prison.

After cadre Do came back, he took over the warehouse so cadre An could take a vacation. I gave her a list of books and cassettes she could find to study further. She was a fast learner. I checked her progress once in a while later when I went to the warehouse to get supplies. I loved her radiant smile with dimpled cheeks. And her crystal voice, so feminine…

Cadre An left Nam Ha camp not long after I was released in 1985. I learned from friends who were released a year after me that she was transferred to work at Noi Bai Airport. It was the big international airport at the vicinity of Hanoi. She must have had good connections and she made a plan, taking advantage of learning English free with me. Good for her.

Perhaps cadre An had love feelings, not pity about me; but I couldn't risk myself. At best, I would've become tangled into a mess that my mother disapproved. My mother was a hardcore against communism. At worst, I would've got tangled into the espionage world. I had heard rumors that the US government was negotiating with Hanoi for the release of political prisoners since 1982. The rumors came from visiting families in the South. They secretly listened to broadcasts by the BBC (British Broadcasting Corporation) and the VOA (Voice of America). Cadre An might have become a setup by the Communists to infiltrate into America. As an intelligence official, I had to think of that possibility. No way could I fall into that trap, although I couldn't forget her.

<11>

12-   The Small Catch

In June 1975, the Communists cast their big net to catch all South Vietnamese government officials and military officers into "re-education" camps all over Vietnam. I was a fish in that big catch, and later I learned that the Communists continued to use their net for smaller catches. As I came out of Section F (Special confinement) of Ha Tay camp in February 1978, I met and became friend with Hau, who was caught in one of those small catches.

Hau was a sergeant in the army of South Vietnam when President Minh declared unconditional surrender to the Communists on the morning of April 30, 1975. He was guarding a post on the Saigon perimeter. He saw chaos spreading fast. People were running panicky in every direction. American helicopters circled hurriedly here and there in the gloomy sky. All kinds of noise surrounded him. His platoon leader shouted in anguish, "Dismiss and run for your life!" Hau ran and took his uniform off at the same time. The streets were full of frantic people and trash. He ran back to his parents' home in the suburb of Saigon. His parents saw Communists tanks passing by. Many of their neighbors ran either to the airport or to the harbor looking for ways of fleeing. Hau's parents thought they would be all right in the new regime. They only owned a small grocery shop and Hau was not an officer. They thought they were just ordinary people in any regime. They decided to stay put.

September 1975 came and Hau's family experienced a blow to ordinary people like them. The Communist victors announced the change of money system. Five hundred South Vietnamese (SVN) dongs (Dong: name of monetary unit) would be replaced by one North Vietnamese (NVN) dong. The amount limit for change for each family was 100,000 SVN dongs. It took just a minute to realize that they could not change the rest of the money they had saved for years. All families in the South now became equal in wealth: 200 NVN dongs in the pocket. It was robbery in broad daylight. On the state-run newspaper and radio, the Communists announced their victory of breaking down capitalism. Hau's family tasted bitterness the first time in their life. They lost the capital to keep their grocery shop going.

Saigon, now called Ho Chi Minh City, lost its economic vitality for the second time. Ten days earlier, it suffered the first attack on big capitalists. All commercial buildings were seized, owners were arrested, and their homes were confiscated. These big capitalists were labeled as "blood-sucking, and labor-exploiting" elements that had to be eliminated in the new socialist society. Hau heard rumors that several owners just jumped right off the balcony in anger and distress. For Hau, his life was more miserable every day. First, he had to give up his Honda motorcycle because gasoline was not available to the public; then he was told to live a "self-sufficient" life, "free from being slave for commercialism."

A year later, in November 1976, Hau witnessed the Communists' direct blow to his family. His parents were invited to a "re-education on small businesses" class for two days. At the end of the class, they were told to voluntarily give up all their merchandises to the state-run co-op. Local authority assured Hau's parents that they would get paid as employees! Another robbery in broad daylight. Hau felt he had enough of Communist propaganda. He needed to do something to vent his anger and frustration.

His parents endured the hardship to live on because of their children. Since Hau was the oldest child, they wanted him to take their gold to make an escape by sea. During his search for a connection he could trust, he stumbled into something better: the National Reconquering Force. Yes, he was a soldier; he could be a soldier again.

Hau had wandered around the city to do odds and ends for survival. He had a favorite stop for lunch. He made several acquaintances with whom he could share his misery. He noticed a middle-aged man who liked to sit at the table next to his. The man seemed harmless as a Pedi cab driver. One day, the man introduced himself as Mr. N and invited him to his home for a drink after work. Hau came a few times. He saw Mr. N lived by himself in a poor little house made of coconut palm leaves in a dark alley. He learned that Mr. N lost his wife and children during the evacuation from central Vietnam in March 1975. President Thieu had ordered a tactical military withdraw and it became a panicky rout, foreboding the collapse of South Vietnam. After a few sips of rice alcohol, Mr. N leaned forward to whisper into Hau's ear:

"If you said that you were a South VN sergeant then Sshh, I am a South Vietnamese lieutenant colonel in hiding."

"Why didn't you escape, Sir?" Hau almost made a salute but Mr. N stopped him fast.

"I have a secret mission. Nah, you are too young to join. Forget it, just pretend you didn't hear, OK?" Mr. N tapped Hau's shoulder, "We're friends; that's enough."

"I am old enough! I had two years in the army. I want to join your mission." Hau felt his blood was boiling. The rice alcohol was making him hot, too.

Mr. N. nodded his head. He shook hands with Hau. To show that he trusted Hau, he flashed a few pictures of his past wearing the rank of a lieutenant colonel. He even flashed a picture of him with the secret leader, a two-star general in hiding. The general did not flee when Saigon collapsed. Hau didn't dare to question Mr. N. because Mr. N. had now become his superior. Hau was given the rank of a lieutenant and he would be in charge as a platoon leader soon to be formed. Mr. N. did not ask for Hau's money. That part was taken care of with the secret fund from the general; and the general got the money from the Americans.

"You don't need to know much. Just remember the American Seventh Fleet is still out there to support us."

"Wow! How promising!" Hau thought.

In early 1977, Mr. N gave Hau a moving permit issued by the district police where he lived. He was to go to My Phuoc Tay village in Go Cong Province for the secret opening ceremony of Mr. N's new regiment. "The permit is fake; don't show it, not even to your parents," Hau was told. Mr. N. said that the general was hiding in the swampy jungle nearby. Again, Mr. N reminded Hau that the hide-out location was chosen because it was close to the sea, easy access to the Seventh Fleet just in case.

The ceremony was held secretly in a thatched- roof house at the end of the village. Hau met a dozen other officers in Mr. N's regiment. Everybody was tense and serious. Mr. N explained that he could not make a larger group for the ceremony because he was afraid of being exposed and discovered by local authority. Mr. N was in South Vietnamese army uniform with his rank at the collar and his pistol by his hip as he stood in front of them. He praised all his patriotic officers as the leadership frame for the regiment. He asked them to solemnly take the oath in front of the Fatherland altar. To conclude the ceremony, Mr. N took out a military radio and tuned in to connect with the general. Hau's spirit soared as he heard congratulations from the general. Mr.

N then gave each officer a pistol and only one drink of rice alcohol,

"We saved the party for victory," he said.

Mr. N insisted Hau and others to stay overnight in the house as it was too late to leave the village. He was staying with them, too. Hau gently slipped his pistol under his pillow with a pounding heart. The victory seemed so near, he could feel it before he lay down to sleep.

Hau woke up to a shout and a flashlight. The nozzle of an AK-47 was pointing at his face.

"You are under arrest," a security policeman shouted.

Hau got up and looked around. Others were being handcuffed like him. The world crumbled at his feet. On the way out of the house, he and others noticed that their regiment commander was not with them. They were caught red-handed of a conspiracy against the "People's Revolutionary" regime. Their weapons were evidence against them. In the court, the witness to their crime was Mr. N, now wearing the Communist police uniform as a captain.

In October 1977, Hau and others like him were put on a ship to go north. The local authority at My Phuoc Tay was filling the quota set by a higher level. Hau ended up to Ha Tay camp. He was in the brick-making team with me. I was glad to share my ironic title "Highly-talented young man" with him. He got his rank as a lieutenant in just a few hours and now he was in prison with high ranking officers.

It took me a while to hear his whole story. I made fun of him when I said,

"Now you know everything he showed you was fake, except the moving permit, right?"

<12>

13-   Choosing The Wrong Door

Hoa was in the brick-making group with me at Ha Tay camp in North Vietnam in 1977. He was a pilot captain in the South Vietnam Air Force. He wasn't in the big catch (Story #2) by the Communists as I was, nor was he in the small catch (Story #12) as Hau was. He ended up in the Communist concentration camp because he chose the wrong door at a critical point in his life. His story made me laugh bitterly because he was at the door to heaven then he turned his back to go to hell instead. The price for believing in Communist propaganda was eight years in prison for him (1975-1983).

When President Minh of South Vietnam announced the total surrender to the Communists around 10:30 AM on April 30, 1975, Hoa was flying his Huey chopper on a mission in the MeKong Delta region where the South Vietnamese military strength was still intact. The whole crew of eight didn't want to surrender. They voted unanimously to flee, so Hoa turned the chopper out to sea. He landed on an American war ship of the Seventh Fleet. He and his crew were ordered to push the chopper into the sea to make room for a bunch of other choppers waiting to land just as he did. Hoa realized the war was over, and his family was left behind.

Hoa was brought to a refugee camp in Guam in June 1975. He spent day after day looking for his family in the big, noisy and frustrated crowd. He couldn't find them.

Instead, he found a group of people who were separated from their families now wanting to return to Vietnam. The group was more vocally demanding each day. Hoa particularly remembered a member of the South Vietnam Congress. This congressman preached patriotism. He demanded Guam authority to return him and others to Vietnam. Hoa didn't like the congressman himself, but he joined the congressman's movement because he saw his chance of reuniting with his family. He got sucked into the sweet talk of national reconciliation and the sweet sound of a warm welcome to the "run-away children" returning to the Fatherland. He knew they were the Communist propaganda slogans in the war; somehow he thought the Communists meant it after the war. During our talk, he even argued with me:

> "You see, the war was over. After the American Civil War, the Yankees didn't treat the Confederate soldiers badly. After World War II, the Americans didn't treat the Germans or the Japanese badly. Why would the Communists treat me badly when I bring my heart and my brain back to them?"

Hoa made a big, big mistake.

As the "Homeward bound" movement grew over a thousand persons, a South Vietnamese Navy officer agreed to lead a Vietnamese commercial ship back to Vietnam. The ship belonged to "Viet Nam Thuong Tin" (Vietnam Commercial Credit) Bank. It left Saigon on the last day of the war. The ship got hit by a Communist B-40 mortar on the way out but made it to Guam. Perhaps the Navy officer thought that he was giving the Communists a big present and he should be rewarded. Well, he got 13 years in prison for his patriotic act.

Before letting the "Viet Nam Thuong Tin" ship leave, the American authority in Guam had repeatedly persuaded people to rethink their choice. Over 1,600 people, including Hoa, insisted on leaving. The Americans then gave them everything they needed: food, clothes, housewares, beddings, and medicines. On the day of departure, the thoughtful Americans even gave them the last chance to make their choice: Hoa was instructed to go into a small room by himself. At the other end of the room, Hoa saw two doors, one for going back to Guam and the other for boarding the ship. Being alone in the room, Hoa was under no one's pressure to make his decision. The majority of people (1652 persons to be exact) chose the door to the ship; only a few chose the other door to go back to Guam for freedom.

I interrupted Hoa while he was talking:

"Did you see the leading congressman on the ship?"

"Nope. He chickened out," Hoa said bitterly; then he added, "I'll punch him hard if I ever see him again."

After two weeks, on September 29, 1975 the ship reached Vung Tau, the seaport at the mouth of Saigon River going to the city of Saigon. Although the South Vietnamese Navy captain had contacted Vung Tau Port Authority in advance, the ship still had to wait a full day before someone approached them. The Communist greetings were far from a warm welcome. Hoa and other people on the ship sensed the hostility of the new regime, but they were stuck. The ship was almost out of fuel.

The "Viet Nam Thuong Tin" ship was escorted by two former South Vietnam war ships to go north to Nha Trang in the central coast, about 250 miles from Vung Tau. It was ordered to anchor off shore. The Communists then sent out small police boats to unload people and take them directly to the interrogation center. Instead of a hearty welcome, Hoa was greeted with a cold stare on the hostile faces. He was ordered to abandon all his clothes and belongings for inspection. He was given two pairs of prison clothes in exchange for all the things he had.

Every person on the "Viet Nam Thuong Tin" ship had to go through Communist interrogation. Hoa was considered as a suspected CIA agent. The Communists thought the ship was a CIA scheme to put a Trojan horse on their land. All of the people on the ship were denied family contacts. Women and children were released after nine months. More than five hundred South Vietnamese officers were shipped north in late 1976. They were deemed more dangerous than their fellow officers inside Vietnam. They had left Vietnam and they chose to come back, therefore, in the Communist mindset, they got to have a spy mission with them.

Hoa remembered he had to explain over and over again why he wanted to return to Vietnam. During an interrogation, the Communist cadre asked him:

"What mission did the CIA give you when you were alone in the departure room?"

"Nobody was there to give me any mission!" Hoa exploded.

"That showed how clever the CIA is! They taped the mission. You listened. The tape self-destroyed. Do you think we are stupid?" The cadre fired back, and then he said,

"We will get to the bottom of this. We don't want any more ships like yours."

"Then why you broadcast your national reconciliation policy?" asked Hoa.

"Hah! That's for people we can trust. Not you. Anyway, don't you know that it's better to imprison a wrong person than to let a criminal slip away free?" He snorted.

Hoa vowed that he would never trust any Communist words again, nor would he listen to any sweet talk about Communism.

<13>

14-   The Grave Digger

Love is powerful. Love combined with a strong will is even more powerful. I witnessed that kind of love in an extraordinary situation.

It was mid-1979. I was in a Communist concentration camp in Ha Tay, North Vietnam. The Communists couldn't hide the political prisoners in the north any more. Boat people who escaped Vietnam exposed to the rest of the world the miserable conditions and whereabouts of more than fifty thousand political prisoners who were secretly transported to the north in 1976. To improve their image to the world, the Communists began allowing visits from family members of the prisoners. Wives traveled more than a thousand miles from the south to see their husbands. The trip took three days and three nights on an old, rickety train. Their first visit was limited to no more than fifteen minutes.

We prisoners who were doing hard labor, saw the wives once in a while in the reception huts. We weren't allowed to talk to them and the guard who escorted us had his AK-47 ready to shoot. If we were lucky, we would see the wives on the road, coming in or leaving the reception huts. A bittersweet mixture of sadness mixed with joy always accompanied these rare encounters. A feminine image from the south was so wonderful, a much welcome break from our harsh reality.

I first saw the lady while two fellow prisoners and I were pulling an ox cart to carry clay from a field outside the camp to our brick-making group inside. I saw her when I was on my way out of the camp while she was on her way in. She was carrying big bags on her shoulders and hands, like many other wives. It was just past noon and humid hot. I could see sweat running down her face and I noticed a big birthmark under her left ear. We exchanged quick glances and nods. She seemed to recognize one of us because she said Hi. We heard the click of the rifle from the escorting guard as the warning. Silence filled the moment. We felt so close yet so far…

That night, I learned that she was the wife of Lieutenant Colonel T. in the Special Police Force. He was in the same hall with me, but not in the same ward. It was the last time Mrs. T. saw her husband. He had been ill and malnourished for many months but only one herbal drug was provided for all illnesses in the prison. The food and medicine she brought was too late to save her husband.

I saw people die almost every week since I was brought from the south in 1976. The dead person was put in a makeshift coffin made by political prisoners of the carpentry group. The body was then carried away by criminal prisoners to be buried on the slope of a hill outside the prison. The field where we got the clay to make bricks was on the opposite side of the road from that hill.

Three years later, in 1982, I happened to meet Mrs. T. again on the road. My two teammates and I were still digging and carrying clay by the oxcart to our brick-making group. The rules had been relaxed somewhat since her previous visit three years earlier and I could exchange greetings with her. She came with a young man in a communist army uniform. I wasn't as friendly with her as I would've liked because of his presence. Mrs. T. quickly explained that the army man was her son. I wondered how the son of a political prisoner was able to get into the communist army. That seemed unlikely and I wasn't sure I believed her. I noticed he was also carrying a large bag. They came to visit her husband's grave. I understood that she had come to do the standard ceremony to end the three-year mourning period.

Mrs. T. and her son headed to the cemetery on the hill after reporting to the prison command post. I guessed she must have visited the grave before. They were up there for several hours. On our last trip for the day, around 3:00 PM, we could still see them on the slope. Strange... The ritual usually didn't take more than an hour as we had seen on other occasions. Besides, visitors had to leave the camp by 2:00 PM to catch the last bus back to Hanoi. What Mrs. T and her son were doing seemed destined to remain a mystery to me forever.

To my utmost surprise, I saw Mrs. T. again for a third time in 1996. I was working as a window clerk at Oakland Claremont office of California Department of Motor Vehicles. I couldn't mistake Mrs. T.'s distinctive birthmark. She waited in line until she could come to my window because she needed someone who could speak Vietnamese. After helping her, I asked if I could meet with her away from the DMV office on a different day. She agreed. When we met, I had to refresh her memory about me and her last visit to her husband's grave. She was startled. It was, indeed, a small world after all. I told Mrs. T. that I admired her and wanted to know more about what she was doing on the hill that day and how she came to be in my DMV office. This was her story…

Mrs. T. was pushed to the limit in 1982. Her family was shattered when her husband was put into concentration camps and then died. She and her children lived in a residential area that had been reserved for South Vietnamese middle ranking police officers and she was under constant pressure by the local authorities to leave the city. The last straw was the draft order for her oldest son. In previous years, the communist authorities wouldn't accept family members of South Vietnamese officers into their army. But now, the precinct authorities where she lived didn't care any more about her family's connection to the South Vietnam regime because her husband was dead. The precinct had to fulfill the draft quota set by higher authority and they badly needed soldiers for the battlefields in Kampuchea (formerly known as Cambodia). There were rumors about how soldiers from families like hers were used by the communist army. Most likely, her son would be used as a human shield. Mrs. T. had to act fast and take great risks to save her son and her family. She developed an elaborate plan of escape but she wouldn't leave without her husband's remains. She loved him too much to leave him behind.

How could Mrs. T. dig the grave without being caught? How could she carry her husband's remains on the long train ride without being discovered? The answer: her son in communist army uniform, a perfect shield. The soldier was still an image of national hero at that time. She obtained the uniform in the black market.

"Did the chief warden question your son about wearing an army uniform?" I asked.

"Yes. I showed him the draft order." She smiled bitterly, "I fooled him. I said my son couldn't wait to wear the uniform of the best army. He came to beg his father's forgiveness for joining the army that defeated him."

Mrs. T. and her son dug the grave without incident. They washed the bones with rice alcohol right there. I could visualize running tears and sweat mixed on their faces on that hot summer day. That night, they stayed in the village inn near the prison to secretly wash the bones again before heading back to the south. They had to make sure that nobody could detect any odor from the bones in the long train ride.

Once in the south, Mrs. T. bribed people to have the bones cremated. She then had a Buddhist monk bless the urn before embarking on a dangerous boat trip away from Vietnam. The boat ran out of fuel after the fifth day, putting them adrift in dismay in the middle of the sea. They didn't encounter Thai pirates as happened to many of the Vietnamese boat people. Instead, they were rescued by a South Korean cargo ship on its way to the Philippines. Her family and the hidden urn made the escape successfully. Not many boat people got lucky like that. She credited her dead husband for protecting the boat on its dangerous trip.

Purchasing a communist army uniform on the black market was illegal. Removal of her husband's remains was illegal. Cremation was illegal. Escape from Vietnam and Communism was illegal. Any of these acts might have led Mrs. T. to the same fate as her husband. What courage!

I never saw Mrs. T. again. I refrained from getting better acquainted with her because, as she told her story, I could detect pain in her eyes and her voice. My presence was a reminder of her late husband in an awful past and I felt it was important to respect Mrs. T.'s privacy and her love. What an incredible lady!

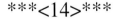

<14>

15-   The Wild Plum

The kitchen group leader patted my shoulder:

"Remember what I told you yesterday. Be safe on your first day and every day; and remember cadre Do's warning: Don't mess around with local people. You're being watched every minute although you feel you're alone in the woods. Now go, and bring back good logs for the kitchen."

I went into the woods for the first time. I was assigned to the kitchen group not long after I was transferred from Ha Tay camp to this Nam Ha camp in 1983. Since then, I had worked in the cleaning team, the cooking team, the coal team and now came my turn to go to the woods. Cadre Do was in charge of the kitchen team. His warning was interpreted by us prisoners as: "Don't think of escaping. Local people will turn you in." Cadre Do knew I was an intelligence official and I had military training, but he still let me leave the camp by myself. "Could it be that he feels I am no longer dangerous or what?" I was wondering.

A fellow prisoner went with me to the woods, but as soon as we reached the foothill he left me. Going together wasn't productive. He reminded me to mark my path along the way although he knew, just like him, I had gone through some survival training while I was in the military school. I took a deep breath to inhale the fresh air of freedom (kind of), and opened my way into the undergrowth with a short knife which looked almost like a dagger. I had two knives for the job: The shorter one was for clearing the way and cutting small branches; the longer one, like a machete was for chopping down the tree. I carried the longer one across my back with ropes.

The dirt road from the gate of the camp to the foothill was about a mile. From there it was an upward, zigzag climb until I could find something to chop down. The local people needed wood just like the kitchen group in the camp so good wood was hard to find. I had to climb up a good while before I could find big trees. Cadre Do set the quota of 40 kilograms (88 pounds) for a day's work. Nobody met the quota that I knew of, but he didn't seem to mind. Usually a big trunk of 1 foot in diameter x 10 feet in length or 2 small trunks of the same length would do, as long as the wood was solid and not white. The white wood didn't burn well at all, as I had experienced. To cook for a camp of two thousand people, the kitchen had 8 big stoves using self-made charcoals. The wood was used to start the charcoals and as reserved fuel when needed.

I enjoyed being in the woods by myself. The work wasn't easy though. I got cuts and bruises. I had no gloves. I wore regular prison clothes. I wore no shoes, only the sandals made from old tires. The hardship became a matter of fact to me after being in prison over eight years. I focused on the things I gained: fresh air, green vegetation and sunshine, the sound of nature from the leaves, the birds and insects. I also found extra sources of food: some edible leaves and wild fruits. To my utmost surprise, I discovered something that would forever be a part of my life journey.

One day, deep in the woods, I was climbing up a tree and reaching out to a branch for some wild fruits when I heard a girl's voice, almost crying:

"Mister, you are taking my plums! Please don't," she was begging.

"They're wild, how could you claim them yours?" I stopped my reach and looked down with surprise and a little fear. I saw a small figure several yards away looking up at me.

"I found the tree and have been tending it a few years. I come to get some plums for my grandpa." She spoke rather softly as if she was afraid someone could hear her besides me.

Feeling safe, I climbed down. Suddenly I realized she didn't have the same accent as the local cadres in the camp had. Her accent was more refined, more civilized and her words were not harsh. I started noticing her look. She was like a little girl, maybe 15 years old. She wore simple clothes, not much better than mine, just different color. Her clothes were brown and mine were dark blue. Her hands and feet were covered with cloth wrapping like a bandage for protection. I saw only her fingers sticking out. She wore a large-brimmed dark-green hat to cover much of her face. I waved my hands as a sign of greetings and good will. She gave me a faint smile.

"Just as I thought, you're a re-educationee prisoner, aren't you?" Her voice was friendlier and she stepped closer.

"Yes, how do you know?" said I, with a surprised tone.

"Your Southerner voice, mister! And your clothes, too." She chuckled. She had a musical laugh, or I thought so. I hadn't seen a girl for a long while.

Duh! I forgot about my Southerner accent. I had heard stories of failed escape because of the distinct accent and the different look of the prisoners from the South. I laughed at myself, too. The girl became friendly.

"My grandpa told me to respect people like you, if I ever meet one. Are you chopping wood for the camp? I've been watching you since you came to my land this morning," She cleared the vegetation at waist-deep and came to me.

"Your land? What do you mean?" I got another surprise.

"Shhh! Don't be too loud." She put a finger on her mouth and looked around. She was hesitant for a minute then said:

"I've planted cassava and yam around here so the village authority can't tax me." She seemed to have enough trust in me to confide her secret. I was moved.

I started getting very curious about the girl. I followed her on her well-hidden path to an area not far from the wild plum tree. She cleverly camouflaged what she grew into the undergrowth. I understood her intention of showing me her land. It meant that I should respect the fruit of her labor. "This girl is not ordinary," I thought.

The girl and I became friends quickly. She wasn't ordinary, indeed. Her grandfather, on her father's side was a French government employee in Hanoi. He was sweet-talked to stay when the French left in 1954 after the Geneva Agreement. The Communists, under the disguise of Viet Minh as a national front to combat the French colonialism, needed his accounting expertise. Once they squeezed out all his knowledge, they threatened to put him in a concentration camp unless he relocated his family. And he bitterly agreed to move because it was too late to flee south. He became a peasant in the village co-op. They forbade him from teaching, especially the French he knew. His children couldn't go to college because of his past, and now his grandkids couldn't go to college either. The girl was 19 at the time but the hard life and malnutrition made her look as tiny as a 15 year old kid. I thought I saw my future through this grandfather's life. My mother had already been sweet-talked to give up her home in the vicinity of Saigon to go back to her hometown in the countryside. The Communists told her I had a better chance of being released with her relocation.

"How old is your Grandpa?" I asked on the second time we met.

"He's seventy. How old are you, mister?" It was her turn to be curious.

"Thirty five."

"I thought you were older," She stopped short as she realized that was not a compliment. "I am sorry," she added.

"Don't be. I'm sorry to hear about your grandpa, and you."

"Yes," She sighed. "My grandpa was hoping you would come to liberate us…" She left her sentence hanging then what she said next would stick in my head forever.

"I have another secret to tell you. My name is Man." She lowered her voice to a whisper.

"That's an ugly name for a girl! It means 'Barbarian'. You know it, right?"

"Yes! And I am proud of it after my father told me his intention when he gave me the name. Don't you get it?" She stood tall.

"He made it ugly to protect you from the devils and bad boys, huh?" I made my guess from the common practice of old people.

"No!" She shook her head fast. "Read it backward, mister!"

A rush of emotions flooded me, gave me goose bumps. I felt a blush of shame on my face, too. Her father was yearning to go South (Nam). Her family was yearning for Freedom. And here I was. I failed him, I failed her grandpa and I failed her personally…

I met the girl a few more times during my two weeks of chopping wood. All of the meetings were brief and in secret as I respected her privacy. For me, I had to find other places for good wood although I loved to see her young face with very bright eyes. I was able to give her some medicine for her ailing grandfather.

Both of us were very sad on our final meeting. The girl handed me a few wild plums from her tree. We held hands for a long minute then she turned away and left hurriedly. I thought I saw tears in her eyes.

The girl was quite a wild plum herself.

<15>

16-   The Beginning of True Love

I have two big lovers in my life. The first one was Dieu. She became my fiancée after the fall of Saigon in 1975, and then she left me while I was in Communist concentration camps. The second one, Tram became my wife in 1986, one year after I was released from the camp. I had known Tram before Dieu, but the twist and turn of events proved that Tram was meant for me.

I was released from prison in January, 1985 and stayed in Saigon, trying to rebuild my life. One morning in February, 1985 I rode my bicycle to the state-run pharmacy where Tram worked as an accountant in Cho Lon, the Chinatown of Saigon. I asked her to take a quick break for a talk. As soon as we sat down at a corner table inside the coffee shop, I looked at her playfully. I refrained from reaching for her hands.

-"Whose money is it that you bought the materials for my pants and shirts?"

"My money," answered Tram softly with an apologetic look. "Please don't feel offended. I am making good money. Brother An told Mom about your situation after prison time. She likes you. We all do. We want to help you. This is not pity. Please don't feel that way. Please let us help you through this hard time."

The continuous flow of her words showed that she had prepared for this meeting. A week earlier, Tram met me at the home where I stayed temporarily and gave me the materials. She came with one of her sisters. She said her mother was happy to hear of my release and told her to give me the materials for new clothes. That visit was brief and I felt it was rude to talk about money in the initial meeting.

"Tram, I am not offended. I thought it was your mom's money…" I was hesitant to continue what I was thinking. I stopped and stirred the freshly-made lemonade drink that was just brought to me. I was trying to find the next words.

"Mom wants you to have the materials and bring them home so sister Vi can measure and make the clothes for you. Mom wants to make a connection between you and sister Vi."

There! Tram said it for me. I felt so relieved. This girl was able to read my mind.

Suddenly, the crush I had on Tram when she was 12 years old came back to me. I was overwhelmed with indescribable feelings. I realized instantly that I had to seize the moment or forever shut up:

"Tram, I don't have any chemistry with Vi. It's you that I do! Don't you remember how many times I came to see your brother and ended up playing and talking with you? Don't you remember how I took your photos in the summer of 1970, when you were twelve?"

I spoke what I had prepared since she came to give me the clothing materials. During that short visit of hers,

I found out that she didn't have a boyfriend. The old flame was rekindled in me.

"I had no idea!" exclaimed Tram and her face was turning pale, "I remembered your look was very strange when you took pictures of me in that summer; but I thought you were using me as a bridge to reach sister Vi. Everyone at home thought so. My grandma and my mom said openly that you and sister Vi would make a perfect couple!"

Tram stopped short to sip her drink. I could see her right hand trembling slightly holding the spoon. I knew she was being caught off guard.

"No, Tram, it's you that I've had my eyes on."

I reached for both of her trembling hands. I looked deep into her eyes and intertwined her fingers with mine,

"It's you that I've been thinking about all along. Now that you are old enough and have no boyfriend yet, can I see you often?"

I refrained myself from saying "I am in love with you" because I wanted to give her time to make up her mind on a man who had nothing to offer her.

Years earlier, when I came to say goodbye to her family in 1967 before I left for America to study, I had asked her parents for a picture of Tram and her youngest sister. I put that picture on my desk because I just loved the dimpled smile on her beautiful young face.

I was sure that by now, Tram knew of my situation. I came out of Communist prison after ten years with nothing in my hands. My fiancée left me. I stayed in the city illegally because I didn't want to report to my mother's hometown in the countryside. Under the Communist rules, as being single, I had to be with my mother; but my sister came up from the countryside to tell me not to go home. She had very bad treatment from the village authority after she was released from prison near the end of 1977. My sister was a first lieutenant in the South Vietnam Army.

Tram left me with her pale face and trembling hands to go back to work. She told me later that her co-workers noticed her unusual appearance. It took Tram the whole day to calm down and she made up her mind: she accepted my first lunch date with her a few days later. She insisted on treating me to a good meal though. The street where she worked was well-known for a dish of steamed chicken with ginger-flavored rice in some Chinese restaurants. We didn't have to go far. I had the best meal since I got out of prison. The food was good, but Tram's appearance was what I remembered. She looked lovely with the short hair showing her marble neck. The short-sleeved shirt and pants were tailored just right to show her curvy, youthful body. Her eyes were sparkling, her dimpled smile was radiant, and her voice was so sweet. I thought I saw all the signals for my next move.

During the lunch date in the following week, I told her the reason why I stopped seeing her family after I came back from America in 1971 and began working. Her grandmother called me upstairs one day. She wanted my parents to come and have a talk with her about the marriage arrangement for Vi, Tram's oldest sister and me. Vi is four years older than Tram. That scared me away because I never had any chemistry for Vi. I knew that I could never admit my crush on Tram. There are five girls in the family and Tram is the fourth one. The first three had to get married before Tram became available. That was how things worked in the mindset of Tram's grandmother and no one could challenge her authority. Tram's oldest brother, An made a perfect example of obedience when he accepted the marriage arrangement by their grandmother.

Tram listened to me while eating, half surprised, half amused. She said I was a "dirty old man" when I told her how I took her hands into mine while we were in the movie theater in the summer of 1970. That year I was allowed one trip home during my scholarship years in America. Of course I had to ask for her parents' permission, and I had to take her youngest sister along for the movie. I teased her about being too innocent to sense my crush. She teased me back that she was glad for being innocent, or else she had to travel a thousand miles to see me while I was in concentration camps in North Vietnam.

After lunch, I made my next move: I asked Tram to go see a movie with me. To my pleasant surprise, Tram nodded her head. She timidly gave me a signal to wait when we were back in front of the pharmacy where she worked. She went in and out in a jiffy and off we went.

We didn't really care what Communist film it was. We just went into the nearest movie theater from her work place to save her time (or were we too impatient to be together privately?).

I was 37 and Tram was 27 at the time, but we were like a bunch of kids again not long after we sat down in the dark theater. I was nervous and excited. I could sense her nervousness, too when I slowly put my left arm around her shoulder. I could feel the goose bumps on her left upper arm. My right hand reached over her lap and touched her nervous hands. She was frozen stiff. Her face was looking straight to the screen but she was trembling warm. I used my left arm pulling Tram closer to me, and used my left hand to turn her face to me while my right hand hooked around her waist. In a few seconds, I felt her resistance then suddenly our lips locked together and our arms closed in. My ears became oblivious to everything around me. I never forget that first kiss. My wet lips pressed hers hard and my tongue was dancing madly around her confused tongue. Time stood still. I was in heaven.

The kisses became more frantic and breathless as my right hand started to unbutton the middle of her shirt to feel outside her bra then underneath. Tram was twisting her body to avoid my touch but she was moaning softly at the same time. I was being rewarded for ten years without touching a feminine body. The agonizing hunger for the opposite sex dissolved fast. My crush for Tram was real and big, huge, enormous…I felt like I could feel

Tram forever if the light wasn't turned on. I saw Tram's embarrassment as she quickly gathered herself while I was feeling ecstatic. Her look was loving and even more charming. If we came into the theater as a man followed by a girl a few steps apart, then we came out as a couple holding hands.

The first seemingly easy steps weren't so easy afterwards. Like a good cook that kept me going back for more, Tram was able to control my carnal urge for her body and turn my lust into the lasting love I have for her. I couldn't reach further down on her virginal body until we were engaged and she resisted my seduction until we had the wedding. My mother and her mother were on her side all along. They constantly kept reminding me that sex had to go with love.

Tram has become the better half of me since then.

<16>

The Double Ugly Ducklings

All Vietnamese names have meaning. My wife knew a lady who named her two sons Tuan(for Handsome) and Tien (for Progress). The neighborhood children called them Tun and Tin. The sound "un" and "in" in Vietnamese is equivalent to "oink-oink" in English for pigs. The Vietnamese don't think of pigs as a pet. On the contrary, a pig is considered a lowdown dirty animal despised by people. Tuan was born in 1968. Tien was born in 1969. They were ridiculed openly by the children around because they are half American, half Vietnamese. The adults were more indirect, calling Tuan and Tien as half-breeds or children of dust.

Their parents are Vietnamese, one hundred percent. The father is a crippled veteran. He lost his right leg in battle. He was at home helping his wife as much as he could with chores and took care of the children, four of them. Good father. There are two boys older than Tuan and Tien. These boys were born while the father was still a soldier at his prime. Things changed drastically with the father's discharge from the army. The wife became the breadwinner. She was frantically looking for jobs because her husband's veteran benefits were next to nothing. And she happened to get a cleaning job at an American compound near Tan Son Nhat Airbase in the vicinity of Saigon, capital of South Vietnam.

The rule at work was that she could only clean vacant rooms. One day, the lady was doing the cleaning and the American soldier returned to his room for some reason. He looked at her, smiled awkwardly then he hesitantly took out some green in his wallet to show her. She fought a desperate battle and she lost. Just once, she told herself, just once. The money was good though. She was able to buy more things for the family. She was happier and she became pregnant in no time. Her happiness ended at the minute the nurse, with a grim face, carried the newborn baby to her. He had black skin. How could she face her husband? Should she give him up or keep him?

The bad news reached the father the same day. Two days of silence followed. On the third day, the father sent the news that he wanted to keep the newborn and ordered his wife to go home, no second thought. The lady wept with remorse. She told herself: No more.

The lady promised her boss the same. She was back with her cleaning job. In just a few months later, she got pregnant again. This time she was pretty sure that it wasn't her husband's baby, but she didn't have the heart to do the abortion. It was her baby regardless. Money, duties and responsibilities somehow mixed in with lust. She blamed herself for her weakness at the same time she felt compassion for the lonely, homesick American soldiers. They were young and she was still in her prime. Another black baby added to the family. Again, the father was tolerant. He silently blamed himself. He swallowed his pride to keep the family in one piece.

The lady's parents weren't tolerant this time though. From the countryside in the Mekong Delta, southwest of Saigon, they rushed to the city to apologize to their son-in-law for giving him a bad wife. That's Confucianism. Parents are responsible for their children no matter how old the children are. The lady was ordered to quit the job, and bowed before the husband to ask for forgiveness. Very sad time, but everybody agreed on one thing: keep the baby.

Tuan and Tien grew along with the other brothers. The two older brothers were taught to protect Tuan and Tien from being bullied by children around. There were fights and quarrels almost daily until one day, Tuan and Tien were able to protect others in his neighborhood against children from another neighborhood. Being bigger and stronger, Tuan and Tien beat their opponents easily.

Then came the event of April 1975. The Americans evacuated big time. South Vietnam lost the war to North Vietnam. It wasn't a civil war. It was a Communist triumph over American imperialism. Tuan and Tien, in their innocence, joined other children to celebrate the victory on the streets. They jumped up and down. They joyfully waved the communist flags until someone with a red band on his right arm shouted at them:

> "*My den* go home! *My den* go home!" (*My_den* in Vietnamese means Black American)

And the crowd turned itself onto them with pushing and shoving. Suddenly, Tuan and Tien realized they had a different skin color that they forgot about. They were frightened. They cried and they ran back to their home as fast as they could while the poisonous words followed them:

"Remnants of imperialism! Go home or die!"

The father couldn't hold his tears, seeing Tuan and Tien collapsed behind the door and cried loudly. They have been ugly ducklings since they were born, and now, it was double ugly. He sent words to his parents-in-law in the countryside. In an urgent family meeting, the adults agreed that Tuan and Tien had to go hiding in the countryside until the anti-imperialism sentiment toned down. Their mother hugged them in her arms as tears flowing freely. She brought bad luck to the family the day they were born. Bad luck now became double.

In the countryside, Tuan and Tien turned out to be big help to their grandparents and the peasants. As they grew older, they grew bigger and much stronger than an average Vietnamese boy. They carried double load on the rice fields. They had no problem working in the mud with their long legs. They were taught swimming and fishing in different weather conditions. They were taught to listen to different sounds that different fish make underwater. They became well-liked in the village, although the village authority looked at them with hostile eyes. Until one day…

It was near the end of 1987. The grandfather was told to report to the village committee at once. Fear fell upon the family. It got to be something related to Tuan and Tien as the summons indicated. The village official greeted him with a broad smile that wasn't often seen on his face:

"You go tell your daughter to take her half-breeds back to the city. We can't allow them to stay here anymore."

"Why, sir?" The grandfather puzzled to hear the order mixing with the smile.

"Why? America wants them. We got directive from central authority in Hanoi yesterday. We can't believe it, but it's in black and white. Order is order." The official sighed.

The grandfather noticed "America" in the official's sentence. It isn't "American imperialism" as he used to hear.

It took a few minutes for the grandfather to realize the full effect of the news. His eyes were swelling with tears. The tears of joy! He rushed home to let his wife know, and they got Tuan and Tien ready to leave. Fairy tales do come true. No more muddy rice fields, no more long hours under the hot sun or monsoon rain, and no more being despised…

Tuan and Tien's parents got the news right away, too. Everything suddenly turned sweet and so bright. The neighbors came with open arms. Some even hugged Tuan and Tien, called them sons. They were offered money and help to get the identification cards and passports. The Communist government became so friendly and speedy. Tuan and Tien weren't fully happy though. Their father insisted on staying in Vietnam. He was glad to see the happy ending for his family, but he chose to stay. He had been humiliated by the neighbors. Now he could be a proud parent. He had to stay to enjoy the feeling of pride instead of leaving to be a dependent. Deep down in his wife's heart, she understood her husband's decision and she respected that. It was time for separation. It was time for closure on her unfaithfulness. The oldest son would take care of his father. That son was rejected by the American officials because he was over 21 years old and married.

The interview, the health screening and the visa processes were swift. The mother and her three boys came to America in 1988 under The Amerasian Homecoming Act of 1987 by the US Congress. They were sponsored by World Vision International to come to California. Being 20 and 19 years old and without any education, Tuan and Tien ventured to Louisiana to work in the fishing industry. The mother and the older son stayed in California.

My wife and I sometimes come to visit the mother in San Pablo, California as she was my wife's neighbor back in Saigon. We often listen to her complaints that her two older sons do not help much while Tuan and Tien send money to her and her husband every month. They give their parents half of their wage so their mother and father could have a comfortable life. And they promise to seek parents' approval when they find the girls they could marry. They are more pious and dutiful than their Vietnamese older brothers.

TDUD

BLACK APRIL

The end of the Vietnam War
A bad leader, a grave mistake
Saigon in chaos
An army collapsed in anguished surrender.

The world turned upside down
Freedom lost
Property was seized
Everything belonged to The State.

Long live Communism!
Food was rationed
Garments were regulated
Hammer and Sickle dictated.

Hail Socialist Equality!
AK-47 ready, who dared to protest?
Down with Capitalism!
The defeated South returned to the Stone Age.

APRIL 30, 1975

Part Two:

My Journey to Freedom

MY JOURNEY TO FREEDOM

INTRODUCTION

I am a baby boomer of 1948. I wasn't born in the United States, but my fate has been tied to America since the Americans started getting involved deeply in South Vietnam in the sixties. President Kennedy was my idol when I grew up, and his famous words still hold true in my life: "Ask not what your country can do for you; ask what you can do for your country."

Fate brought me to America as a scholarship student in February 1967. I studied at California State College at Fullerton, and I had my golden time. I came back to South Vietnam in July 1971 and soon became an intelligence official. I "went down with the ship" as South Vietnam fell into Communist hands in April 1975. Of all 105 students in the USAID (United States Agency for International Development) scholarship program that year, I was the only one who got stuck in concentration camps for ten years. I was released in January 1985, from the little prison to the bigger prison: the Communist society. I thought my life was doomed forever with all the restrictions I had to obey.

Fate then brought me back to America again in March 1993 as a refugee under the Humanitarian

Operations (HO) program by the American Government. It was like a miracle. I can never thank America enough for giving me a chance to start my life again. Not only was I an outcast if I stayed in Vietnam, but my sons wouldn't be able to enjoy the freedom they now have. The Communists considered me as trash and America opened its arms to give me a state job to support my family. I have rebuilt my life as an American citizen. I was so proud when my younger son became a US Marine in July 2008 and served in Afghanistan in 2010.

I have all kinds of memories, ups and downs, in my life. I was a poor kid before I enjoyed the college life. I was a high ranking intelligence official before I hit the bottom of the dungeon as a war criminal. I came out of concentration camps with nothing in my hands and then I got the money that my American godfather left me after his death. Most of all, I never forget the memories of being treated as an outcast in Vietnam versus the feelings of becoming an American citizen.

Along with memories are the lessons in life. I learned lessons for being naïve when I first started looking for jobs, then lessons of survival when I was down to nothing in concentration camps and in Communist society. There were also lessons of dealing with people, friends and foes, in many different situations. And yes, I have had lessons in love, too.

I retired from state service as of May 1, 2013. I feel the need to write my life story after my retirement. First of all, I need to keep my brain active, then the need to share my memories and lessons with my family and close friends. I feel like I have been a witness of history, and I am obliged to share what I have experienced.

I always consider myself as a traveler in life. I have picked up quite a few pebbles here and there along the way and now it is the time for me to pass them on…

> *Time is like an eternal road*
> *A traveler suddenly appears*
> *Walking…Falling…Walking…*
> *Until dust become of him.*

My early years

I was born in February 1948 in the suburb of Saigon, South Vietnam. My earliest memories were about the evacuation of North Vietnamese to the South after the Geneva Agreement in 1954. Vietnam was divided into two parts: The North belonged to the Communists and the South was under the Nguyen monarchy with the protection from the French. Behind the French was the visible coming of the Americans. I had new kiddo friends from the North with a totally different accent that was hard to understand at first. I had a vague idea that their families moved south to escape Communism.

In 1955, I started my first year in elementary school. I remembered I had to learn French as my first language. Things changed the following year when Mr. Ngo Dinh Diem abolished the monarchy by a national referendum.

He became the President of the Republic of Vietnam (RVN). The French disappeared from the streets. I saw more Americans and their CARE boxes with the American flag and the RVN flag along with the handshake. I started high school in 1959 and I had English as my second language. I enjoyed a few peaceful years in the atmosphere of a young nation. I was uplifted with patriotism and the idealism of Western democracy.

November 1963 was the tragic month in my memory. President Diem was killed in the coup d'état on the second day and President Kennedy was assassinated on the twenty second. My heart was especially broken on the second event because President Kennedy was my ideal image of a leader. I became aware of political turmoil and the growing presence of American troops as the war spread in the following years. The Communist Uprising had started in Ben Tre Province, my parents' hometown. They kidnapped and killed my uncle who was an outspoken landlord against them. My mind was set to defend my country against Communism when I grew up.

I reached the high mark of my adolescence years when I was chosen to take part in the National Contest at High School Level in June 1966. As the top student in my class, I represented my high school to compete in History and Geography. My teacher, Mr. Ti gave me his best knowledge as my special tutor and lent me his big Rand McNally Atlas to take home for studying. I handled the Atlas with love and fascination. I thought I did well on the geography test. In six hours, I wrote an essay of 10 pages to compare the Great Britain and Japan. I draw about 5 sets of maps for illustrations with color pencils. My writing was done with a handle and nibble dipped in an ink pot. I wasn't allowed to use ballpoint pens. I was lucky to win the First prize in Geography and received a scholarship from USAID (United States Agency for International Development) to study abroad.

My college years, 1967-1971

I left Saigon on February 22, 1967 for America. My feelings of stepping on board the Boeing 707 of Pan Am Airlines were indescribable. I saw and tasted heaven. A whole new world was wide open in front of me. I came in the group of 105 scholarship students that were soon divided into seven small groups after a week of orientation in San Dimas, California. I came to California State College at Fullerton (CSCF) in Orange County. The smell of orange grove mixed in with early morning dew was forever fresh in my memory. After the first six months of learning English, I started my four years of college, majoring in Geography. Those years were the best time in my life and I was able to make some lasting friendship.

1/ Gerald was one of my roommates in Othrys Hall I, the dormitory for boys when I came to Cal State Fullerton. I was put in a room with three American students to maximize my contact with English language and American culture. I still remember that Gerald and I had so much fun talking with our hands in the first few months. One morning, I woke him up as I was so excited:

"Gee! I spoke English in my dream! Wow! I was arguing with my English teacher!"

"Did you, really? You don't like him that much?" He was mumbling in his half-awake state of mind.

"That's not my point." I tried to express my excitement, "I can now speak English without thinking first in Vietnamese."

"Really! Is that so?" He showed astonishment in his eyes now.

Gerald took for granted that speaking English was something natural until he met me. He was very patient in helping me learn English. Being four years older than me, Gerald was my mentor.

Gerald became my American best friend through time. While we were in college, Gerald used to take me in his Volkswagen bug to his home on weekends. His family lived in Rialto, California. He knew I was homesick. He let me stay overnight at his home so I could enjoy the family atmosphere. Gerald's parents were so kind and loving that I felt attached to them in a short time. I called them Papa and Mama. Papa had an infectious chuckle. Mama made the best pancakes in the world. I usually went to church with Gerald's family on Sundays in their golden Oldsmobile. I loved to hear his sister, Suzie sang during church service. Gerald's family gave me a lot of the warmest memories of Easter,

Thanksgivings and Christmas times. The festive decorations, the aroma of food, and the family's laughter were timeless in my mind.

I learned my driving with Gerald. During the weekends at his parents' home, Gerald took me on Papa's truck out to the country roads and taught me driving. He was very patient with me because the truck had stick shift. It took me a while with all the sweating to handle it. It was quite a thrill. Once I could handle the truck, the world was wide open in front of my eyes through the truck's windshield.

I came to know some girls in Othrys Hall II through Gerald. During open house at the end of the semesters, he took me to visit the girls' dormitory next to ours. Suzie, Gerald's sister was there with her roommates. We had so much fun with decoration, food and games. Julia, one of Suzie's roommates later became Gerald's wife. I watched the beautiful love growing between Gerald and Julia after Gerald and I moved out to apartment once I became 21 years old. We had many Vietnamese meals together with my sloppy cooking. I introduced them to bean sprouts and soy sauce. We had so much fun together as we dressed up for Halloween and went trick-or-treat! Then the kayaking at Newport Beach was memorable as I stepped on sea urchins with my bare feet.

I was very sad when Gerald and Julia, as a couple, saw me off at the Los Angeles International Airport in July 1971. As a dutiful citizen, I returned to South Vietnam after my graduation.

2/ Dr. Morrison was the godfather of three students: Sung, Kham, and me. There was no official adoption. The three of us just became his favorites through time. We called him Doc for short. He used to be a sailor in the US Navy during World War II. After the war, he went to college under GI Bills and got his Ph. D in Psychology. He was a counselor when the group of fifteen USAID scholarship students came to Cal Poly San Luis Obispo in 1967. Sung and Kham were in that group.

Doc was single. We were told that he got married when he was young; unfortunately, his wife died while being pregnant. Doc became so sad that he decided to stay single. We respected his loyalty to his wife so much that we didn't dare to match him with anyone, although he had a few pretty colleagues.

I met Doc the first time through Kham, my close friend, around December 1967, when they stopped by Fullerton. Doc was taking a group of Vietnamese students from Cal Poly San Luis Obispo on a trip to Southern California. After that, he used to stop by to see me on his way to seminars in Orange County or Los Angeles City. For me, every long holiday or break that I came up to see Kham, I stayed in Doc's home.

Not long after getting acquainted with us students, Doc learned that we loved the Mercedes car as it was a symbol of prestige in South Vietnam. One day, he traded his American car for a brand-new, light blue Mercedes 250 SL. Doc let us use his new car to take our driving test. We had so many trips on that car with him. We loved to be behind its steering wheel. The Mercedes lived up to its reputation. When Doc took the car for 100K maintenance, he only had to change two spark plugs. The car didn't have bucket seats on the front row, so Doc could take up to ten of us to go steal strawberries on the fields at night or go catching clams and abalones at the beaches nearby. By sitting on someone's lap, we students just piled up into his car. We had so much fun. Those were the days that seat belts were unheard of.

I was as carefree as I could be. I lived a life of a scholarship student. Everything was taken care of by someone. Doc saw that and he gave me and others like me some early warnings once in a while,

> "You are in an affluent society. Don't take everything for granted."

His warnings did not really have much weight until I was thrown into real life; especially when my world turned upside down.

We had so many fond memories with Doc, especially about food. He wasn't a stranger to exotic food due to his extensive travelling during the sailor years. In his home, he allowed us to cook Vietnamese food (very smelly sometimes). He was the one who showed us the anchovies in the American supermarkets. We were able to make the dip with anchovies to go with beef to his liking. Every time we came to San Francisco, Doc would take us upstairs on an old, narrow wooden staircase to an authentic Chinese restaurant in Chinatown. We loved the special rice porridge there. The flavor was just like the one we had back home in Saigon.

It was about the time of our graduation in 1971 that Doc became taciturn. He took some time to be alone with me one day, and I guessed he did the same with Sung and Kham. That day, he asked me about my plan for the future. He respected whatever my plan would be; he just pointed out the options I could be interested in. The first option was staying low at his home for five years then he would help legalize my stay. The second one was going to Canada, and the third one was finding an American girl who would marry me. Sung chose to go to Canada while Kham and I chose to return to Saigon; both of us were pretty idealistic at the time. We knew Doc wasn't happy to see us leave. He started smoking again (He quitted smoking when Sung and Kham moved in with him in 1968).

3/ The Dunnings were Kham's friendship family while he was studying English in Fullerton. I had a different friendship family, but I was invited to Kham's all the same. Gradually, I became closer and closer to the Dunnings.

The friendship family program was the work of the Foreign Student Counseling Office at Cal State Fullerton. They reached out to local people to make foreign students less homesick. The Vietnamese group of fifteen students was chosen by random to be with different American families in Fullerton. Outside the classroom, I had no choice but speaking English with my three

American roommates. During the weekends, I spoke English with the friendship families. I learned English fast.

Dr. Dunning was very kind-hearted and simple. He was a sailor during World War II. After the war, he went to college under GI Bills, and got his Ph. D in Physics (Nuclear Physics, I think). He worked for a company in connections with NASA. When we students found out about his achievements as a rocket scientist, we called him Dr. Dunning with admiration. That kind of calling made him embarrassed quite a bit. He told us, "No big deal" and he preferred us calling him by Abe. Anyone could call him Mr. Dunning and he never corrected that.

Mrs. Dunning is as simple as her husband. She was very active with community and charity work. Besides helping foreign students, she helped typing in Braille for the blinds under the sponsorship of Cal State Fullerton. Like Abe, Mrs. Dunning preferred us students calling her by name, Lisa.

The students were invited to come to the Dunnings for any occasions. We loved to gather at their home. We had so many fond memories at the Dunnings' home, including memories with their children and later, their grandchildren. I still have a special photo with Abe as the two of us were the only ones left at the table. Actually, I was the last one still eating and Abe sat down to join, helping me from being embarrassed.

4/ The Allisons was my friendship family starting around the first month of my coming to Fullerton in

1967. Mr. Allison was a professor of photography at Fullerton Junior College. Mr. and Mrs. Allison have three sons: Bill, Keith and Ted. Bill was on duty in Vietnam at that time. We talked a lot about the Vietnam War when they invited me to spend time with them. I tried to convince Mr. and Mrs. Allison that Bill was doing the right thing for the Vietnamese people, but I felt I wasn't very convincing when the Allisons saw the Tet offensive in 1968 on television. We all rejoiced when Bill came back home alive later.

I had many sweet memories with the Allisons, too. They took me home for weekends, holidays and special occasions. I also went out with them to the beaches and to some special events at Fullerton Junior College with Keith and Ted as they were about the same age with me. I still remember the Allison's Volvo, another well-known luxury brand besides the Mercedes that I admired.

My first job, 1971-1975

I returned to South Vietnam in July 1971 as a dutiful citizen. I became an official in the Central Intelligence Organization (CIO). I felt it was my fate to work for intelligence. If the words "Presidential Executive Office" lured me in, then the word "Geography" paved the way.

I got my BA degree in Geography and I intended to come back home to be a teacher. I wanted to promote the American education system. When I got back, the

Directorate of Mobilization gave me six months to find a job before they drafted me. I had been exempt from military duty during my college years. I was eager to apply for a teaching job at the Ministry of Education. The answer they gave me was a splash of cold water in my face. They would give me a post as a teacher at a junior high school in a rural area for a few months. When draft time came, I had to serve in the military at least two years before I could petition to come back to the teaching post. I wasn't treated equal to someone trained by them. A graduate from the Saigon College of Pedagogy would be assigned to a teaching post at a high school in Saigon vicinity and would be exempt from military duty after the basic military training. I learned a hard lesson in life: I came to apply for a job without any symbolic gift as expected; and I met a resistance wall because I was American-educated while the officials were French-educated. I paid a dear price for my naiveté and arrogance.

One evening when I came home, my father handed me a note for an appointment on the following day. It was for a job interview with someone from the Central Intelligence Organization. I was frightened and I refused to meet the man. A week later, my father told me again that someone wanted to meet me. The way my father described the man suggested that my father didn't want me to refuse this time. According to my father, the man was a real gentleman in a nice suit carrying a business attaché case and driving a car. The man introduced himself as the Director of Research from the Presidential Executive Office. He wanted to offer me a job that would fit me as a graduate from an American university. I accepted the appointment but I wondered about the location of the interview. It was a house in the suburb of Saigon, nowhere near the Presidential Palace.

I showed up for the appointment and met the man. The man was articulate and praised me for being a good student. He said I was the kind of person he needed to help him analyze aerial photographs, meet with foreign dignitaries and, above all, to listen and translate public addresses by the American Presidents so he could report in a timely manner to the President of South Vietnam. I was sweet-talked into accepting the offer. The man shook my hand and left to let another man prepare the necessary documents with me.

When the paperwork was ready and presented to me, the second man spoke slowly to make sure that I understood every word,

"We are agents of the Central Intelligence Organization, disguised under the name of the Presidential Executive Office. You are in our safe house. You may refuse our offer, but after you walk out of here, we cannot guarantee your safety."

I sensed the threat in his words, *"Work for us or else!"* That was it.

In the first week at my job with the CIO, the head of the personnel bureau showed me a memorandum from the US Embassy. The memo asked the South Vietnam government to recruit graduates from USAID scholarships. The Director at the CIO was interested in me because my major fitted nicely into the undercover title. In the paperwork that sent me to the Ministry of Heath for medical check-up, it stated me as "High ranking official, class A, Geography specialist for the Presidential Executive Office."

I had 14 weeks of basic military training from January to April, 1972 before I was assigned to the Bureau of Intelligence Research on North Vietnam Politics. I learned to collect data and information, overtly and covertly, on North Vietnamese political leaders. I learned to write weekly and monthly reports with the American CIA reports as guidelines. I came to love my job as an intelligence research agent.

The most intense time was the month of October, 1972 when President Thieu didn't agree with the original draft of the Paris Agreement. He went on the air to denounce the draft as a sell-out to the Communist demands. Viet Cong (the counterpart of North Vietnam in the South) would be present in South Vietnam's infrastructure from village level and up. My Bureau was ordered to be on 24/7 duty over a month to analyze each word in the draft and each spoken word by North Vietnamese leaders. I worked in coordination with the President's special task force to revise the draft. President Thieu then gave the revised draft to President Nixon and what followed was the 12 days of B-52 bombing in Hanoi. The Paris Agreement was signed on the 27th of January 1973.

In October, 1974 I was promoted as the Bureau Chief of Intelligence Research on North Vietnam Politics. My position was equivalent to a major in the armed forces. I worked for the CIO until the last day of South Vietnam on April 30, 1975. I wasn't evacuated, neither was the whole CIO due to extreme chaos at the end. I spent the next ten years in the Communist concentration camps.

The years in darkness, 1975 – 1985

I accepted the fate of "being sunk with the ship." In the last meeting with my superiors at the Directorate of Intelligence Research on April 26, 1975, my superiors repeated the words of President Huong who took the office after Mr. Thieu fled, "Fight to the end". With the presence of the American advisor, the Chief of the South Vietnam CIO confirmed that the Americans had a plan to evacuate the whole organization. I dutifully obeyed orders and waited for evacuation. On April 29, I heard the song "White Christmas" on the American radio channel. That was the code for total evacuation. Unfortunately, the evacuation for my organization was never materialized as chaos spread fast. Anyway, I was told to keep working regardless of evacuation or not because there was hope for a settlement as General Big Minh took office from President Huong on April 27. I was told not to destroy my working files. That foolish hope didn't live long though. General Big Minh surrendered to the Communists around 10:30 AM on April 30, 1975. I lost my job and I was stuck.

In June 1975, after two months to give the Southerners a false sense of reconciliation and to consolidate their victory, the Communists started the round-up. They made the announcement of "a re-education period for 30 days" for the mid-level to high level of South Vietnamese government officials and military officers. This 30-day period became three years and beyond once the Communists got everyone into their fishing net!

The entire South Vietnam CIO was taken to a camp that used to be an orphanage village (how ironic!) in Long Thanh District, about 40 miles southeast of Saigon. Yes, I felt like an orphan once I lost my fatherland. My organization was one of the four groups being held at Long Thanh camp. The other three were: The Special Police Force (ranks of major to general), the Administration sector (rank of deputy chief of district to deputy Prime Minister), and the members of various political parties (in central committees).

Around October 1976, the North Vietnamese Communists erased Viet Cong, their South Vietnamese counterpart (so-called South Vietnam Liberation Front and its Provisional Government), to unify Vietnam under the sole Communist rule in Hanoi. Two thousand prisoners from Long Thanh camp were transported to the North along with high ranking officers in the South

Vietnam army. The total shipment was estimated around 50,000. The reason for shipping prisoners north, in my opinion, was the fear by the North Vietnamese Communists that their disgruntled Southern counterpart might release the prisoners to join force in fighting against North Vietnam. Indeed, a few big names from the Southern fraction were upset and fled to France.

The vast majority at Long Thanh camp were transported by trains and ships. I was one of the few exceptions. I was taken to Thu Duc camp where the South Vietnamese military officers, up to generals, were held. I was among those prisoners to be transported by airplanes (the C-130 Hercules) that had been abandoned. Such an irony for me when I got on board the plane with one hand carrying my bag of belongings and the other hand was handcuffed to the hand of another prisoner. I used to fly in that kind of plane with soldiers around to protect me as a special agent to do field interviews on high-ranking defectors.

Not long after being taken to Ha Tay camp, about 20 miles south of Hanoi , I remembered one night, during a regular session of "re-education"; the cadre told us prisoners to read a special piece of news from the Communist party newspaper. The news was about the release by the Chinese Communists of their last prisoner, a general, from the 1949 revolution in China. The cadre emphasized that "Revolutionary forces are always lenient to those who opposed." I made a quick calculation in my head. That general from Chiang Kai-Shek's army was captured in 1949 when the Communists took over China mainland. Now he was released in 1976. Twenty seven years later! Wow, he just had enough time to take a few breaths of the outside air before going to the graveyard. It would likely be the same fate for all prisoners like me.

I went into the darkest period of my life in December 1976. One night, I was taken to the confinement quarter. It was known as section F, where the American POWs were held earlier. Each cell could hold up to six prisoners. The sleeping arrangement was a simple concrete platform with just enough space for six straw mats. Each mat was one meter wide (1 meter= 1.09 yard). The gate was heavily guarded and closed at all times except for a brief moment, twice a day, when meals were delivered. I felt honored to be in the same cell with Brigadier General Nhu, the last Police Chief and four other high ranking officers of the Special Police Force.

This was the time of intensive interrogation. The Communists were very suspicious about the post-war scheme by the Americans and my organization. I wasn't tortured but I was under extreme stress as I had to answer all questions verbally and in writing day after day. Many of these questions were very complicated and all of the questions were asked many times by different interrogators. No doubt that the answers were compared and scrutinized for details. Many times the interrogation lasted all day, and then the writing for weeks. The Communists insisted that I must have been an American

135

CIA agent because my last position was Bureau Chief of Intelligence Research on North Vietnam Politics and I was educated in America. The confinement period lasted fourteen months before they moved me back to the regular ward. They assigned me to the brick-making group (making bricks for the prison and making it literally from raw clay in the field to the finished product).

While I was in confinement, I was allowed to write letters home once in a while with a box office address as the Communists still kept secret of the political prisoners' whereabouts. I wrote several farewell letters to my fiancée, who is my close friend's sister. I told her not to wait for me as I expected to be in prison indefinitely. She is Kham's sister, my love since 1973. She agreed to go with me for evacuation in 1975 and I failed her.

Around June 1978, I came to the lowest point in my life. An interrogator cornered me. He openly accused me as a CIA agent. In my spurt-of-the-moment defiance, I wanted to prove my innocence once and for all by committing suicide. I wasn't successful in the attempt. The Communists seemed to treat me better after that incident though. They gave me books from American and European Research Institutes on military strategies and political strategies to translate for them. I seized the opportunity to show them that the Americans and the Free World were far better than their Soviet and Chinese allies.

I remembered the year 1978 as the most miserable time in prison. We prisoners were on the verge of collapse after three years of starvation. There was no rice in our meager meal, only corn, potatoes, millet or cassava. Family visits were not allowed. All kinds of sickness were treated with only one herbal medicine. Death from hunger and sickness happened weekly in every ward. I witnessed my fellow prisoners dying next to me. The irony was that during such desperate time, I often dreamed of being back in America. I remember two particular dreams: I was rescued by helicopter in one dream; in the other somehow I was able to sneak through an airport fence and aware that I was free on American soil at last. Such were sweet dreams to face harsh reality!

Through the family letters that were screened by the camp cadres, we had hints that the outside world was very miserable, too. If the letter said "our home is very clean now"; that meant all furniture had been sold to get food, for example. It took us prisoners a while to figure out the meaning when some letters said "the children were sent to go fishing and they caught big fish." That meant the children were sent out to the sea to seek freedom and they were rescued. Boat people became known to the free world after the Vietnamese Communists took extreme measures to erase capitalism in South Vietnam. They eradicated big businesses and small businesses altogether on behalf of the people. South Vietnam became a big co-op. They also changed the South's monetary system: 500 old units were exchanged for one new unit and each family was allowed to have only 200 new units. The rest of the family's savings became plain paper, just like that. Glory to the Socialist Equality!

In early 1979, God saved the political prisoners taken to the North when the Chinese Communists waged a short-term war into Vietnamese provinces along the Northern border to teach the Vietnamese Communists a lesson. China felt insulted when Vietnam toppled the Cambodian regime backed by China in 1978. As a precaution, all high-ranking South Vietnamese military officers who were in prisons close to the Chinese border were suddenly and hurriedly transported south to the camps in Ha Tay (where I was being held) and other locations around Hanoi. The relocation of prisoners, to my opinion, was deemed necessary by the Vietnamese Communists because they feared China would free the prisoners to make a deal with the Americans. They also feared China would make a big announcement to the world about the inhuman treatment and the number of prisoners, which had been kept secret.

Ha Tay camp became more crowded but the prisoners seemed to see the light at the end of the tunnel. International human rights organizations began to pay visits to the camp in late 1979, thanks to the world's outcry about boat people; and the rumor spread that the US government began talking with Hanoi about taking the political prisoners. The international visits were kept secret from the prisoners. I remembered there were signs when a human rights group was about to come: half the straw mats were ordered to be hidden, the screaming sounds of pigs being killed in the kitchen, and the cadres hid prisoners in wooded areas out of sight from the camp. Then everybody waited for the sound of bells to return to camp. Prisoners were not required to work on the day an international group visited and prisoners were given a meal of white rice and some pork. It wasn't much of a meal but it was a feast for an "orphan" like me (an "orphan" was jargon for a prisoner whose family couldn't come to visit him). There was no meat and no white rice in the daily meal in prison, except on big Communist holidays and on the Lunar New Year. As for family visit that was allowed in mid-1979, a certified hard- labored prisoner would get two family visits a year. For me, my fiancée left me and my mother couldn't afford a long trip of more than a thousand miles to the north. She could only send me two packages of necessities a year; each weighed 5 kilograms (1 kilogram=2.2 lbs.)

Starting in 1980, I witnessed the change in attitude of the camp cadres and the guards. They became friendlier and the regulations were more relaxed and flexible. The war with China in 1979 was a factor. They were taught earlier that the friendship with China was unbreakable; now they learned that China became enemy number one in state newspapers and on state radios. The hatred towards American Imperialism faded away fast in the Communist propaganda. The second factor was the family visits from the South to see the prisoners. The camp cadres and the guards were shared things that they never had before: Western cigarettes, Zippos, soap, shampoo, perfume…and especially Western medicines that worked wonders on them. We prisoners were soon allowed to cook at night for tea and coffee parties. We played and sang our pre-1975 music inside the ward. The cadres and the guards sometimes stopped by outside the iron bars to have a sip of tea or coffee with us inside. They even discreetly revealed that we prisoners had become their "strategic reserves" as the rumor spread openly that Hanoi was negotiating with the American government for our release.

In March 1983, I was transferred to Nam Ha camp because Ha Tay camp was ordered to relocate all political prisoners. Nam Ha camp is a little further south from Hanoi than Ha Tay camp. I was put to work in the kitchen. The work was harder but I was better fed. Off and on I taught English to the cadres who supervised the kitchen team. To me, I had my chance of proving "Who is triumphant over whom?" In 1975, the Communists used that slogan in their lectures to "re-educate" us prisoners.

A risky move in 1985

I was released in January, 1985. In the release certificate, I was sent back to the countryside where my mother was, in Ba Tri District, Ben Tre Province (the so-called "Cradle of the Revolution.")

When I left home for "re-education" in 1975, my parents were in the suburb of Saigon. After my father's death near the end of 1975, my mother was tricked into return to her hometown so her children in prisons could be considered for early release. Upon returning to her hometown, my mother got the decree (which she called a verdict) from the People's Committee of the village to confiscate all the land that she and my father inherited. The decree stated that my mother *"came from a landlord family, became a landlord herself, and had children working for the puppet regime."* Before leaving for America, I asked my mother to give me that decree as a keepsake.

My younger sister, a first lieutenant in the South Vietnam army, was in prison for two years (1975-1977) before she was released to be with my mother. She was under very strict regulations and observation. She had to report to the village authority weekly and kept a journal to show them. She couldn't leave the village even a day without their permission (She was house-arrested several times for violations). She had to do community service when needed, and it was often needed. On the Communist holidays, she and others like her had to go to the village's police post to stay overnight because the local authority didn't want any demonstrations or sabotage acts to happen. I got all the above information when I first arrived back in Saigon and, through a relative, I secretly asked my sister to meet me for a briefing. My sister's last words before leaving me were:

"My brother, don't ever go home."

I began thinking of ways to stay in Saigon, which was now called Ho Chi Minh City. Kham, my close friend from college days took me to the local police station where I petitioned to stay in the city for two weeks. The reason for staying was the need to look for my lost mother after ten years in "re-education" camps. The reason I fabricated was credible and the security police officer approved it without asking any questions. I started my uncharted journey in blind faith that things somehow would work out for me.

After two weeks at my friend's place, I had to leave because I didn't want to trouble Kham further. In fact, his younger sister was my fiancée and she couldn't wait for me. I didn't blame her a bit as it was I who wrote farewell letters to her when I was in confinement, losing all hope. I started wandering around the city with the bicycle Kham gave me. I stayed at relatives and friends, each one a day or two then moved on because no one wanted to risk helping a "re-educationee" like me. They would be harassed by the police if I was caught staying illegally in their home. I fully understood that I was an outcast and I could be back in prison if I was caught failing to report to local authority after being released. I tried hard to swallow the bitterness in a world turned upside down.

To those who live in the free world, how the Vietnamese Communists controlled the society in the 1970s and the 1980s may be difficult to comprehend. Each family was registered as a household and given a voucher for food and necessities each month. For rice, the range was 9 kilograms (equivalent to 20 pounds, 1 kg=2.2 lbs.) per month for children and the invalids, 15 kilograms for a working person. For meat, each family was allowed to buy one kilogram of pork or chicken per month. Beef was for the privilege only. White sugar was rationed at one kilogram per family per month. No full stomach meant no demonstrations and no uprising. Fish, fruits and vegetables were plenty as South Vietnam is in the tropical zone. Outside the rations at government-controlled price, there was black market for everything. Gasoline was also for the privilege. It was a time to sell any valuable things for necessities. It wasn't unusual to visit a friend and see his house without sofa, tables, beds…The Communists turned South Vietnam back to the Stone Age until the bamboo curtain was gradually lifted in the late 1980s.

The household registration certificate served another important purpose: to control people's movement. At least once a month, the security police officer who was assigned to a block would check each household to make sure no strangers mix in. Any visitors had to be reported within 24 hours, and any trips outside the city limit had to be approved by the local government at each end of the trip.

The Love that kept me going

I came to the high school re-union party at the end of January 1985 to celebrate the Lunar New Year. I met An, my best friend in high school again. He told me to come home with him that night. I wasn't a stranger to his family. I came to An's home many times when we were high school buddies. Sometimes I stayed the whole day. I liked his two youngest sisters, especially Tram, for her dimpled smile. She is ten years younger than I am. During my college years, I had a picture of Tram and her youngest sister on my desk. In the summer of 1970, when USAID allowed me one visiting trip home, I saw Tram and I had a crush on her. Of course I couldn't say anything because she was only 12 years old.

The seventh day of that Lunar New Year in 1985 became an important point of time for me and Tram. It marked the beginning of our lasting love. Knowing that I was released from prison, her mother told Tram to buy clothing materials for me. I was told to bring the materials back to her home so Tram's older sister, Vi, a tailor, could make new shirts and pants to save me money. I was moved by Tram's gesture.

During Tram's visit to give me clothing materials, I probed and found out that Tram didn't have a boyfriend yet. The following week, I rode my bicycle to her work

144

place, a state-run pharmacy, to ask her out for a drink at a café nearby. Tram innocently told me to make a move to be Vi's boyfriend. She got the shock of her life when I confessed my crush on her, way back when she was just twelve years old. Here was my confession:

I reminded her about the summer of 1970. I took Tram and her youngest sister to see a movie with her parents' permission. During the movie, I took Tram's hands into mine as a gesture of love, but she was too young to notice. Instead, she was busy chatting with her sister. I didn't dare to make further advance. Tram then remembered during that summer, I gave her a lot of "strange eye contact" and took a lot of pictures of her. The following year, 1971, when I returned to South Vietnam after my graduation I renewed my hope with Tram under the pretense of coming to see An. Well, I was called to go upstairs to see her grandmother. Her grandmother admitted that she had had an eye on me for Vi, Tram's older sister since I left to study abroad. Her grandmother said Vi and I would be a perfect match because our astrological signs in harmony according to Chinese astrology. Therefore, Tram's grandmother told me,

"It is now time to ask your parents to come see me so we can make arrangement for your future."

Her grandmother didn't ask much for the engagement: just eighty pieces of good pastry and eighty boxes of jasmine tea to present to relatives and friends for the occasion. I sweated hard upon hearing that; I said

"Yes, Yes, Yes" to her grandmother, went downstairs and disappeared into thin air. I didn't feel any chemistry with Vi at all, I fell in love with Tram for her eyes and her smile with dimples.

After my confession, Tram began seeing me frequently at that café. When I came to pick up the new clothes made by Vi, her grandmother one more time asked me to go upstairs to see her. I was brave this time because I knew Vi had a boyfriend (not approved by her grandmother and her parents), so I told her grandmother of my love for Tram. Although she would rather see me with Vi, she didn't object as Tram was now old enough.

I went downstairs to report to Tram's mother the conversation I had with the grandmother. Her mother admitted that she had an eye on me for Vi, too; but she couldn't go against God's will, as she saw it. Her mother then told me to stay put with her family, no more wandering. Her grandmother was also OK with that decision. Her father didn't like it though, because he himself came back from re-education camps. Tram's father was an agent for the CIO like me. He spent eight years in prison. Her mother, however, didn't listen to him. She argued that "a person with leprosy wouldn't care more or less if he or she got another wound". Her family had already had her father and two brothers as "re-educationees": An was a first lieutenant in the army with almost three years in prison and Tram's second brother was a first lieutenant in the navy with five years in prison. The family already had black marks with local authorities. She didn't mind adding me to the list.

Tram and her mother started helping me to solve my problems. When the security police officer for the block stopped by to check monthly, her mother bribed him and told him about me. That officer was a VC sleeper before 1975 and he used to be a student at Saigon University. He was sympathetic to my mother's appeal. He let me stay in her home but he emphasized that I couldn't get involved in any political activities against the Communist government. Tram's mother assured the officer that I wouldn't get involved in politics. He then advised me, through Tram's mother, on how to get out of trouble. First, I had to obtain paperwork confirmed that my mother was no longer in Ba Tri, Ben Tre. Second, I needed to prove that I had a stable job before I could petition to stay temporarily in the city.

I began to see the road ahead. My mother and sister agreed to run away from Ba Tri. They went up to a new economic zone north of Saigon. I paid them a visit. I was in tears seeing them in very miserable conditions, but I was unable to help with my empty hands. I came out of prison with nothing in my hands. Tram was helping me financially as she was making good money at the pharmacy. Starting around 1984, the Communist government allowed their pharmacies to buy and sell medicines imported as gifts from relatives abroad.

In March 1985, two months after being released, I got a job with my American college degree. I became a teacher of English for the Center of Research and Translation. Then my mother came to attend the wedding of Tram's youngest sister. There was talk about me and Tram at higher level. Those things made her grandmother gave further approval for me to stay longer in her family. Our engagement took place in May 1985.

I was anxious to receive paperwork from Ba Tri to confirm my mother's household was cut off, but there were signs that the local authority wasn't willing to do it. Unexpectedly, I received a letter from Canada. It was from the old college friend, Sung, telling me something that brought tears in my eyes. God was lending me a hand, no doubt.

In the letter, Sung told me that he was keeping a sum of money for me. Sung followed instructions from the will of my godfather, Doc, who passed away in 1983. Doc knew I was an intelligence official because he came to visit Kham and me in 1973. When Saigon fell into the hands of the Communists, Doc feared for my life. He began smoking heavily, got cancer and passed away in 1983 while I was still in prison. In Doc's will, he instructed Sung to divide the money he left, twenty-two thousand dollars, into three equal shares for the three of us. Sung kept this information secret until he knew for sure that I was out of prison.

It took time to get the money from Doc's will. In 1985, Vietnam was still under the embargo by the United States. The money was transferred to me through black market, or through gifts from Sung (in the forms of imported medicines or used Honda motorcycles shipped from Japan). Tram and I tried various ways to get the money, and we were happy with getting about half of its value. Things started to brighten up. I was able to buy a small house for my mother to move back to the vicinity of Saigon. I also got a Honda motorcycle for me (now that I could afford gasoline from the black market!), and most important of all: To have a decent wedding with Tram in March 1986.

I got help from various people when I had money to pave the way. I got the first and most important document to show that my mother moved legally from the new economic zone back to the city (the document was forged, of course). Thanks to the old household file that she kept, proving that she was once in the city, my mother was able to establish step by step her household status again in the city, and I followed her steps. It took three years to untangle the mess I was in.

At the time of our wedding in 1986, I was still not officially a city resident. I was still "living underground". My mother-in-law had to bribe the security police officer to make connections with the local authority to issue a marriage certificate for me and Tram. My legal resident status started with that document (just like in America: a foreign student who gets married to a US citizen will be granted residency in America, right?)

My residency in the city wasn't that easy though. First, I had to register myself in my mother's household. Then I had to wait two years for the reinstatement of my citizenship before I was approved to transfer to Tram's family household. When Tram and I had children, we were able to detach to have our own household certificate, just in time to submit our refugee applications for departure to America. In 1989, the US government under President Reagan signed an official agreement with Hanoi authority to grant departure to America for those who were in re-education camps three years or more. It was named Humanitarian Operations (HO). I became HO people, and local authorities began treating me differently. Things got even brighter.

Looking back, right after I got out of prison in 1985, I illegally filed my case with the US Embassy in Bangkok, Thailand. A high school friend helped me to fill out the paperwork, and then he sent it for me. The paperwork was sent to a friend in Canada before it reached a friend in California, then it was forwarded to Bangkok. After about five months, I received a letter from the friend in California, in which I got an important document from the US Embassy in Bangkok. The document acknowledged that the embassy got my paperwork and gave me my IV (Immigration Visa) number for future contacts. It was rather fast, perhaps thanks to my American college diploma. I sent them more paperwork as I got married and had children. In 1992, when my family was interviewed by the American officials, all the paperwork I sent to Bangkok was handed back to me. I treasure those documents as keepsakes.

In view of the pre-destined relationship

Before going to the next chapter of my life, it is noteworthy to mention what the psychic readers told me and Tram ahead of time.

1- My psychic reading:

On May 1, 1975, the day after the fall of South Vietnam, I left Saigon to flee for fifteen days, hoping I could escape. The American Seven Fleet was still off shore in Vietnamese waters to rescue fleeing people. A colleague and I came to Ha Tien as the first choice. Ha Tien was a town at the border with Cambodia, where there used to be a flea market for people on both sides. I came and saw that it was now deserted with a lot of barb wires and for sure, lots of land mines, too. No luck then. That very evening, I wandered into the foothill nearby looking for a psychic reader to seek some kind of directions for the days ahead. Ha Tien was known as the sacred land full of psychic readers. I came upon a small house with a thatched-roof lighted by a small kerosene lamp. I knocked and there it was, the home of a psychic reader. The lady in brown looked like a Buddhist nun. She asked me to bow and pray at the altar with incense before sitting with her on the divan. She then gave me a set of twenty cards which looked like Tarot cards. She asked me to shuffle, make a wish, and return the cards to her. Next, the lady divided the cards into five stacks, four cards in each, and asked me to choose one stack with my eyes before using my left hand to pick that stack up without hesitation. I did as instructed. The lady began turning the cards over, one by one, and spoke about the days ahead for me:

The first card was a drawing of a girl waving goodbye to a boy. The boy was leaving but turning his head to look at the girl. The lady interpreted it as a farewell scene. They would never be together again. That was what happened to me and my fiancée later.

The second card was a drawing of a man sitting behind bars. The lady said I would be in prison for a while. I was.

The third card was a drawing of a man in full funeral attire, kneeling in front of a coffin. The lady said I would be in mourning for the big loss of a family member. Indeed. Near the end of 1975, the Communists released some of the prisoners because they needed technicians and specialists with technical know-how to run the equipment, along with those who had Communist relatives. The colleague who went to Ha Tien with me was released. He wrote me a letter, saying that on behalf of me, he "had bowed and prayed in front of the picture of my father on the altar". That meant my father passed away after I left home. When I met my mother ten years later, I learned that my father died of cancer and in his last days, he refused to take food. I also learned that my father never went outside the house after the Communists took over Saigon. He didn't want to see "Communist flags flying in front of his eyes."

The fourth card wasn't understood at the time. It was a drawing of a man in uniform sitting behind a desk. The psychic lady said my future wasn't bad after all and advised me to stay low to get through the sufferings then everything would be all right. The fourth card wasn't realized until 1994, the year I was hired as a state employee at California Department of Motor Vehicles.

2- Tram's psychic reading:

Tram had a similar experience with a psychic reader in Cholon (Chinatown of Saigon). When Tram got a job at a hospital in Cholon in 1977, she was assigned to the typing room within a few months. She learned typing and accounting earlier because her mother didn't want her to sit idle at home after she failed the college entrance exam. The typing room was the place where the hospital doctors stopped by to get their reports typed after their shift. Tram got acquainted with a doctor named Ky. He was half-Chinese and married. His wife gave him all daughters, no sons. Doctor Ky learned that Tram had a father and two brothers stuck in re-education camps, so he offered Tram his help. Every week, when he was on duty for public service provided by the hospital to local people, he let Tram know in advance. Tram then told her grandmother and mother to go see him for medical check-up. Doctor Ky would prescribe imported medicines to them, usually antibiotics and quinine (for malaria) so her mother could send the much needed medicines to her father and her two brothers. Most of the time, the doctors only prescribed local medicines, mostly herbal, to local people.

One day in 1979, Tram was introduced to an old Chinese man who Doctor Ky called Daddy. His father came for a medical appointment and wanted to take a look at Tram. After the visit, the father made a bold prediction to Doctor Ky that Tram would give her future husband all baby boys. Seeing that Tram was single and she liked him, Doctor Ky offered Tram to be his second wife and run off with him to Hong Kong as boat people. Tram refused, even though Doctor Ky explained that Chinese men were allowed to have multiple wives until they got sons to carry their family name to the next generation. He argued further that Tram would become his first wife once they got to Hong Kong because he wouldn't take his current wife along. Tram still didn't buy his reasoning.

There was a big wave of Chinese exodus in Saigon after Communist China waged a short-term war into North Vietnam in 1979. It was retaliation to the Vietnamese invasion into Peking-backed Cambodia. The exodus wasn't official but security police would guard it unofficially to make sure it was a safe departure. In return, the police got gold into their own pockets and they got rid of an element of opposition at the same time. Doctor Ky was planning to join that exodus.

Doctor Ky persuaded Tram to give him one last chance. She should listen to what the psychic reader had to say; so he took her to see the psychic reader. Out of curiosity and with a certain extent of trust, Tram went deep into Chinatown with Doctor Ky. She met a blind Chinese, wearing dark glasses. He was introduced to Tram as a psychic reader by taking pulse (in Vietnamese: Mach Thai To). The blind man gave Tram a piece of paper and a pen, telling her she could draw anything while thinking of what she wanted to know. Once Tram finished drawing, he then took her right hand by his left hand and his fingers started pressing down her wrist to feel the pulse. Meanwhile, his right hand was tracing slowly on her drawing. It took a while for the man to finish what he was doing. At the end, he told Tram a few things, through Doctor Ky's translation:

Number one, Tram had a similar fate as her mother: She would marry a man who already had a wife once. That meant Tram didn't belong to the children of her father's first wife. Tram protested that he was wrong. The blind man calmly told her to ask her mother upon returning home. She was surprised to hear a secret. Her father wedded a wife in the countryside at her grandmother's arrangement; then he ran away to Hanoi and met her mother. Her father's first wife was given money to leave her grandmother's home to start a new life afterwards.

Number two, the relationship between Tram and her current boyfriend wouldn't be a steady one if he left her before the full period of three years. She began taking the blind man's words more seriously as her boyfriend was planning to escape by sea and asked her to go with him. Two months before the full three years, Tram's boyfriend left her to seek freedom. She had to stay behind because her mother didn't agree to pay gold for daughters to escape by boat. Their relationship soon faded away.

Number three, Tram would go abroad with fanfare, not in secret. Doctor Ky thought that prediction fitted his plan nicely as the security police would be watching them leaving and when they got to Hong Kong, his relatives would greet them.

Number four, Tram's future husband would be different from her in many ways. Again, Doctor Ky said Yes, he was Chinese and Tram was Vietnamese. She was meant for him.

Tram still didn't budge. She was skeptical. She thought that Doctor Ky translated the way he wanted it to be because she couldn't understand Chinese. Being a gentleman, Doctor Ky respected Tram's decision.

Tram fully realized the blind Chinese psychic reader was truly good when she met and fell in love with me. She went abroad in fanfare as HO people. Her big family and friends saw my little family off at the airport; then we were greeted and taken home by the Dunning family. Besides, I am different from Tram in many ways:

- I am a Southerner, Tram comes from a Northerner family who evacuated to the South after the Geneva Agreement in 1954;
- I was a good student, Tram was not;

- I am a Catholic, Tram's family practices Buddhism

She told me she realized I was meant for her the night I confessed to her that I had converted to be a Catholic. During the time I was in the same ward with the Catholic chaplains at Ha Tay Camp, I learned their discipline and their strong faith.

For me, I thought my confession would mark the end of our relationship because I knew Tram's grandmother and mother were fervent Buddhists. I didn't know that they had changed their minds about religion.

Tram told me of her mother's story: It was getting near the end of 1976 and her mother still didn't get any news of her father and her brothers. They were being transported away secretly from Saigon. One day, her mother was so desperate that she didn't care where the Lambro (a three-wheeler taxi carrying 6 to 8 passengers) would go. At the end of the trip, when the Lambro driver asked her to get off, she realized the destination was next to the church of the Lady Fatima in the suburb of Saigon. She came into the church, didn't care that she was a Buddhist, and started praying in tears to the Lady Fatima. A week later, Tram's mother got the news of her husband and her sons. She was allowed to send gifts to her husband in the North and make trips to visit her sons in the South. Since then, Tram's mother changed her mind on religion and she persuaded Tram's grandmother to do the same. Therefore, my confession of becoming a Catholic was welcome by her family, no objection at all.

Back to Freedom in 1993

My little family left for America in March 1993. I held my tears until the airplane was completely out of Vietnam's air space, then the tears of joy and sorrow flowed at the same time. The departure meant joy for a second chance to start my life; and sorrow for leaving my fatherland.

In feudal times, anyone who opposed the king was sentenced to death, three generations of that person. The grandparents, the parents and the children were decapitated. In modern times, the Vietnamese Communists didn't decapitate anyone physically, but they did it politically. They checked the personal history of three generations when someone applied for a job (all businesses were state-run) or wanted to study in higher education levels. Tram was an example. She finished high school in 1976 and applied for the college entrance exam. She was directed to three different tables where she had to make a selection. One table was for those applicants with Revolutionary families, one table for those with families working for the "puppet regime", and one for those with families on neither side. Tram failed the test, of course, and she couldn't find a job anywhere until her mother bribed an insider with gold to make a connection at a hospital for Tram to get in. Tram and I had to leave Vietnam so our sons could enjoy the freedom to have a future of their choice.

Except Doc who passed away in 1983, I was able to reconnect and rekindle all my college friendship when I came back to America.

Upon my family arrival at the airport in Orange County in March 1993, Gerald and Julia didn't mind driving over a hundred miles from their home in Redlands to welcome us that night. The moment was so touching that I was in tears. Julia then told me of her dream while I was in prison. She had a dream one night that she heard someone knocking, and when she opened, it was me standing at the door. I think her strong faith as well as Gerald's and others had made my return to America possible. In 2001, Tram and I passed the written test and the interview to become American citizens. Thanks to President Clinton's new law, our sons automatically became American citizens, too. Upon hearing our great news, Gerald and Julia drove all the way from Southern California to Modesto in the north to give my family a big celebration at the home of Suzie, Gerald's sister. From almost half way around the earth, I came to know Gerald and Julia. There must be some kind of divine arrangement from The Almighty.

The Dunnings in Fullerton got words that my family was granted to come to America as refugees in 1992. They immediately expressed their wish to be our sponsors. The American officials who interviewed us to confirm our identities were glad about that because there was no need to find a sponsor for my family. That helped speeding up our departure.

On the day my family arrived at Orange County, California the Dunnings came to the airport to take us home. What a warm welcome! That night, we stayed way over midnight just talking. Lisa showed my family to our room, and there were even toys for our sons. Our first son, Andre was five years old, and our second one, Leon was three. The time we stayed in the Dunnings' home was so special, especially to our sons. We moved out after eight months. Had I known that I would get a good job in the following year in Northern California, I wouldn't have moved my family out.

During the first week after arrival, Abe took my family to the Social Security Administration office in Anaheim to apply for benefits. During the first trip in the car on a rather hot day, Tram and the boys threw up. Abe and I were caught by surprise. We knew better after that, always bringing along plenty of plastic bags on any trips.

Tram got acquainted with American cooking through Lisa. The Dunnings remodeled the kitchen before we came. It was beautiful. I am sure Tram had a lot of memories with the kitchen as well as learning a lot from Lisa.

Thanks to Lisa's connections, I soon got a part-time job as a bilingual TA (Teacher's Aide) at a school district in Orange County. I also worked at an AM/PM gas station.

For our sons, they just loved being with the Dunnings for their swimming pool and the food that Lisa made. Just like our sons, Tram and I loved lasagna and strawberry pie made by Lisa. Very yummy!

The Dunnings' home once more became the meeting place for former USAID students after my family's arrival. Besides parties on regular occasions, Abe and Lisa organized two big ones: a re-union party for me in 1993 and one for Kham's visit from Vietnam in 2002.

In 2008, Leon, our second son joined the US Marines and was stationed in San Diego. He came and stayed with the Dunnings in Fullerton many times during his four years of active duty.

It was a very sad time in 2009 when Abe passed away. Lisa gave my family a big honor when she requested Leon to attend Abe's funeral in full Marine ceremonial gear. Abe came from the Navy and Leon, a Marine, was part of the Navy, too. Lisa was so thoughtful. Then on the following day to celebrate Abe's life, I noticed Kaitlin, their granddaughter, made a beautiful card with the drawing of a big tree. That inspired me to make a little speech as a contribution to the celebration. I was taught in Confucianism that a man must grow strong as a big old tree with a large shade to protect his wife and his children. Abe was a big tree with a large shade like that. Not only he protected his family, but he extended his shade to cover others, including the students and my family.

When Leon came back from Afghanistan in 2010, Lisa gave us quite a surprise by organizing a big Welcome Home party for him. Again, we felt such an honor because Lisa invited her friends and neighbors along with all the students. There must be more than fifty people that day.

For Andre, our first son, Lisa made a special trip north joining Gerald & Julia to attend Andre's wedding ceremony and the reception in 2012. Their presence was so special to us, and Lisa was acting as Andre's Grandma. How sweet of her!

Besides the American friends, I have many Vietnamese friends who helped me through my hard times. Thinh & Quyen from Cal Poly San Luis Obispo are the best among them. They acted as a connection between me and my American friends during my years in and after prison in Vietnam. They were able to leave Saigon before the last day of South Vietnam; then they were able to reconnect with Kham when the Communists lifted the bamboo curtain around 1987. My American friends sent me money and gifts through them because any direct contact would cause suspicion from the Communists. In my letters of thanks, I could only mention that I appreciated their yarns to keep my family warm as Mrs. Allison recalled.

I got another irony once I was back to the United States: Up to the present, I have had recurring dreams of being back in the Communist prisons, especially the time I was in confinement with the generals and the colonels. I couldn't help it and I' m kind of mad about it. Those dreams have prevented me from going back to Vietnam. I thought I would go back to see my mother after I became American citizen, but she couldn't wait for me. I lost both of my parents without seeing them in their final hours.

AFTERWORD

In 2012, I started thinking seriously about writing a memoir when Diane, my DMV colleague, told me about her father's feelings of shame. He is a Vietnam War veteran. He used to be a B-52 navigator on bombing missions along Ho Chi Minh Trail. He felt ashamed of his service because he wasn't welcome back after his duty. I took time to explain to Diane about the war and its aftermath. I showed Diane how her father's work was appreciated by me and others who fought against Communism. The Vietnam War ended but the battle between Capitalism and Communism is still going on as it has unfolded after the Communists took over South Vietnam. I need to write and share my memoir with Diane's father and other veterans. Their sacrifice was not in vain as Vietnam is now open to Capitalism and many North Vietnamese parents are sending their children to the United States for higher education.

Looking back, I see my life as a chain of mixed events, of ups and downs. Good luck turned into bad luck and vice versa. At the time I got the first prize in geography, then a scholarship to study abroad and came back to have a good job, I seemed to have all the good luck in life until the Communists took over South Vietnam. I lost everything. I got myself into hellish situations. I heard comments such as "That's the price for embracing American Imperialism". Who could imagine such bad luck brought me the ticket back to heaven?

THANK YOU, AMERICA!

MINH FULLERTON

__Note:__ Except for political leaders' names, all other names have been changed to respect privacy.

<<>>